Praise for the
OPEN YOUR HEART series

"It's a great idea!"

—Regis Philbin

*"The OPEN YOUR HEART series
is a winning combination
that both instructs and inspires."*

—Hazel Dixon-Cooper, author of *Born On a Rotten Day*
and *Love On a Rotten Day*, and *Cosmopolitan
Magazine*'s Bedside Astrologer

*"The perfect books to improve your mind,
get in shape, and find inspiration."*

—Bonnie Hearn Hill, author of *Intern, Killer Body*,
and the Geri LaRue newspaper thriller series

OPEN YOUR HEART
with *Reading*

Mastering Life through Love of Stories

JEANNETTE CÉZANNE

DreamTime Publishing, Inc.

DreamTime Publishing, Inc., books are available at special quantity discounts for bulk purchases for sales promotions, premiums, fund-raising, and educational needs. Please contact us at www.DreamTimePublishing.com for additional information.

Library of Congress Cataloging-in-Publication Data

Cézanne, Jeannette.
    Open your heart with reading : mastering life through love of stories / by Jeannette Cézanne.
        p. cm.
    ISBN 978-1-60166-011-4 (trade pbk.)
    1. Books and reading—Psychological aspects. I. Title.
    Z1003.C43   2007
    028'.9—dc22

                                                    2007021498

Branding, website, and cover design for DreamTime Publishing by
    Rearden Killion • www.reardenkillion.com

Illustrations by Janice Marie Phelps • www.janicephelps.com

Text layout and design by Gary A. Rosenberg • www.garyarosenberg.com

This publication is designed to provide accurate and authoritative information in regard to the subject matter covered. It is sold with the understanding that the publisher is not engaged in rendering legal, accounting, or other professional service. If legal advice or other expert assistance is required, the services of a competent professional person should be sought.

—*From a declaration of principles jointly adopted by a committee of the*
American Bar Association and a committee of publishers.

This book is printed on recycled, acid-free paper containing a minimum
of 50% recycled, de-inked fiber.

Contents

Note from the Publisher, vii,

Acknowledgments, xi

Author's Note, xiii

Foreword, xv

INTRODUCTION
Flights of Fancy, 1
THOUGHTS ABOUT READING . . .
from Jill and Mandy O'Craven, 4

CHAPTER ONE
Start at the Beginning, 7
THOUGHTS ABOUT READING . . .
from Lady Di, 17

CHAPTER TWO
Storytelling, 19
THOUGHTS ABOUT READING . . .
from Phil Rickman, 31

CHAPTER THREE
Faraway Places, 39
THOUGHTS ABOUT READING . . .
from Anastasia Czarnecki, 53

CHAPTER FOUR
People, 55
THOUGHTS ABOUT READING . . .
from Andrew Wetmore, 63

CHAPTER FIVE
It Was the Best of Times, 69
THOUGHTS ABOUT READING . . .
from Carolyn Haley, 79

CHAPTER SIX
The Butler Did It, 83
THOUGHTS ABOUT READING . . .
from Elizabeth Chadwick, 95

CHAPTER SEVEN
Everything I Know
About Life I Learned
from a Novel . . . , 99
THOUGHTS ABOUT READING . . .
from Karen MacDonald, 107

CHAPTER EIGHT
Fear, Love, and
Everything Else, 111

CHAPTER NINE
Imagination:
Coming Full Circle, 131
THOUGHTS ABOUT READING . . .
from Sharon Darling, 146

CHAPTER TEN
Nonfiction Themes, 149

Conclusion, 157

APPENDIX A
More Numbers, 163

APPENDIX B
Plot Twists and Turns, 167

Resources, 169

Index, 179

About the Author, 187

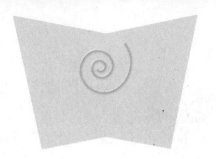

Note from the Publisher

Balancing the overall mission of a series of books with each author's individual creativity and vision is an enjoyable and rewarding challenge. The goal of this note is to tie the loose ends together to make your experience with this book as meaningful as possible.

We have two goals with the Open Your Heart series. The first is to provide you with practical advice about your hobby or interest, in this case reading. We trust this advice will increase your ongoing enjoyment of the printed page, or even encourage you to explore a new side of yourself as yet undiscovered.

Our second goal is to help you use what you know and love to make the rest of your life happier and easier. This process worked in different ways for each of our writers, so it will likely work in different ways for each of you. For some, it's a matter of becoming more self-aware. Just realizing what makes you happy when you're writing, and then gradually learning to use those feelings as a barometer when dealing with your job, relationships, and other issues could be an important first step. For others, reading provides an important outlet for stress and contemplation, allowing you to go back into your daily life refreshed. For yet others, you might discover how to meditate, how to connect with the mysterious flow of the Universe when you are immersed in reading, or the many other ways you can enjoy the printed word. Once you recognize the beauty of that for what it is, you can then learn to connect with the flow in other ways at other times.

We are not suggesting you will find all of your answers in this book. We are, though, inviting you to look at something you love with new eyes, a new perspective, and a new heart. Once you recognize the importance of feeling good in one area of your life, you are open to feeling good in the rest of your life. And that is the cornerstone to mastering your life.

Happy reading!

Meg Bertini

Meg Bertini
Publisher

If you can write the stories for a society,
it doesn't matter who writes the laws.

—AUTHOR UNKNOWN

This book is for the storytellers,
and for those who listen to them.

It's also in memory of King Alfred,
who traveled with books and was committed
to raising the literacy level of his subjects.

And it's especially for Paul,
who makes the stories with me.

Acknowledgments

No book is written in a void, and particularly not one that climbs on the shoulders of so many brilliant and talented writers, poets, and scholars as does this one. So to all of them—and to all those regretfully not included—go my most humble thanks.

Belated thanks to my mother, who passed on to me her imagination and love of words and reading. It is the most profound and important gift a parent can give a child.

To my fourth-grade teacher. When I asked if I could copy out a poem that was read in class, she said, "No, but you can *learn* it if you'd like." All through my subsequent grades at the convent school I attended, I was required to memorize verses, scraps from literature, aphorisms and important pronouncements alike, and every single one has served me well.

To those who made this book happen: Meg, Janice, Brian and Dexter, Helen, and Gary; to Philip Spitzer and Lukas Ortiz, literary agents *extraordinaires:* I appreciate what you all do. Thanks to Derek and MacKenzie at the Squealing Pig in Provincetown and Missy at the Shaskeen in Manchester (for what writer doesn't require a local pub for inspiration, solace, and company?).

I'm especially thankful to two friends who had drifted out of my life for a time (or, more accurately, out of whose lives I'd drifted) and are back in it, both of them women who spark my creativity and feed my soul: Jessica Lupien and Elaine Gottlieb. And thanks to those who give me space and time in Provincetown: Jon Arterton, as always, and Wilderness Sarchild: thank you for the gift of the sea and the community I love.

For help from the CELery: Ann Fothergill-Brown, Geoff Hart, Helen Glenn Court, J. T. Thompson, Karen Lofstrom, Spike Y. Jones, Elizabeth Whitaker, Hilary Powers, Donna Melton, Sara Hyry Barry, Odile Sullivan-Tarazi, Mary Joan O'Connell, Miriam Bloom, Linda Thrasher, Mark Wise, Chris Speakman, Barbara Necol, Sally Noonan, and Carol Eastman.

Thanks to those who let me pick their brains for opinions and literary examples: Alicia Dooley, Carem Bennett, Jessica Lupien, Elaine Gottlieb, and Elizabeth Doherty. And thanks to my historical fiction email list for their help: Kathy Page and Nikki Foster.

Thanks also to David C. Smith of the Library of America, for generously inviting me to explore more literature and for introducing me to Dawn Powell's works.

And of course my thanks always to my first editor and critic, my best friend and husband, Paul. He takes my work out of the domain of "Jeannette's project" and makes it "our project;" and that kind of sharing is my best experience of a true community.

Author's Note

For those who buy into the adage that there are two kinds of people in the world, here's one: there are readers, and there's the rest of the population.

Note that I didn't say, "there are people who read." A lot of people read. That alone doesn't necessarily make anyone *a reader*. A reader is someone who equates reading with breathing. Who will read the backs of cereal boxes, if necessary. Who will walk around the house, tripping over pets and furniture, because she can't put a book down. Who promises himself "one more chapter" but keeps reading until four in the morning anyway.

It's very much an addiction. *Hello, my name is Jeannette, and I'm a reader.*

Because of that, were I to ever put together a reading résumé, it would be eclectic beyond anything rational. Which is just fine with me: Shakespeare's *Tempest* and a graphic novel and the story of code-breaking in the Second World War and a tome on book publicity live happily together on one of my shelves (literally—I just read off the first four titles, starting from the left, and that's what I came up with).

No: I haven't read *everything* Albee wrote (and I'm reasonably sure I don't want to). I'm not even certain that I could spell Dostoyevsky off the top of my head (though, to my surprise, I just did). There's not the kind of depth to my reading that you'd find in a graduate seminar. But I don't read to study: I read to live. And a superficial knowledge of a *lot* of authors has always felt more appropriate than an in-depth understanding of only two or three.

So this book isn't for people who want the depth of a graduate seminar. It's for those who want to read more, who want suggestions for reading, who want to open their hearts to books and all the wonders they contain.

And, finally, for those who may yet learn how literature can open their hearts to much, much more. Thanks for joining me.

I must add a caveat. I am a child of the Western world: my culture and experience are European and North American, and I write out of that knowledge base. I hope that another such book might be undertaken at some time by someone with a knowledge of African literature, Far Eastern literature, Indian literature, and so on, but in the meantime I am limited to the Western canon—and, unfortunately, due to space restrictions, to very little of that even. I offer my apologies . . . and my hope that there will still be something of value here for everyone reading it.

Jeannette Cezanne
Provincetown, MA, and Manchester, NH
Spring, 2007

Foreword

Chicago, Illinois 1975:

A woman—a wife and mother—is shopping for food with which to make the night's dinner. She comes across a second-hand store. She enters. Inside the store is a box. Inside the box is a collection of books. She carries the box of books to the counter, and after a bit of haggling, she convinces the owner to let the books go for two dollars. She brings them home to her children. Sets them down on the living room floor. She tells her two boys they should go look in the box to see if there is anything they would want to read. One of the boys goes off into his room. Plays with his basketball. The other makes his way toward the box. He opens it. A plume of dust rises into his eight-year-old face. In the box he finds: A four-volume set of the *Abridged Encyclopedia Britannica* (only four years out of date), three romance novels (in which he has absolutely no interest), Isaac Asimov's *Before the Golden Age* sandwiched between *The Raven*, by Edgar Allan Poe, and *The Complete Works of William Shakespeare*.

Since the Poe is the shortest of all the books, he opens it first:

Once upon a midnight dreary, while I pondered weak and weary,
Over many a quaint and curious volume of forgotten lore,

He pauses. There is something in the sound of the words. There is something moving in his brain. He continues to read.

> While I nodded, nearly napping, suddenly there came a tapping,
> As of some one gently rapping, rapping at my chamber door.
> "Tis some visitor," I muttered, "tapping at my chamber door—
> Only this, and nothing more."

"Nothing more?" he says to himself. "What do you mean, nothing more? There's got to be *something* more!"

For him, it has begun. He is hooked—there is no turning back.

This personal recollection of my entry into the world of the printed word will cause no surprise to any avid reader. Oh, I had of course read books before, such as the Golden Book Series and the like, but nothing so grabbed me, so "thrilled me—filled me with fantastic terrors never felt before" as did *The Raven*. I read it. I re-read it, and have now had the pleasure of reading it to my children.

For me, and I suspect for most who have had the fortune to have been guided to Jeannette Cézanne's *Open your Heart with Reading*, reading is more than *fundamental*—it is *elemental*. Books are essential to our self-perception, and not to have them limits our access to beauty and dreams (imagine the world of *Fahrenheit 451*). Conversely, when we have unfettered passage to what the world's great books contain, that is, the stories of our species, we begin to "shuffle off th[e] mortal coil" and are renewed.

Open Your Heart with Reading is a rallying cry for the necessity of a lifelong intimacy with the word. Through this intimacy we experience both our individual and collective selves. This simultaneity brings us to a greater understanding *humanness*. (Who has read *The*

Scarlet Letter and *not* better understood stoicism through Hestor Prynne? Or learned the awful wages of anger-turned-obsession from *Moby-Dick*?) *Open Your Heart with Reading* reminds us that great books are companions who, if we allow them to walk with us, will instruct us throughout our lives.

Cézanne's writing is both well wrought and accessible. Her scholarship is informed by decades of intense devotion to writing and her subject—but is also imbued with the wisdom and epiphanic clarity our Disney-Colbert-Dr. Phil-ified society hungers for. *Open Your Heart with Reading* is a spiritual journey as well as an intellectual one.

Cézanne, however, does not only instruct us through her own intellect and wisdom. She, like any good teacher, inspires us by allowing other writers to speak to us about what we all love. Whether it is Phil Rickman who answers the question "why do you read?" with his own questions: "Why do I eat? Why do I breathe?" or Carolyn Haley answering the same question with "How can I *not* read?" These writers continue to confirm the simple truth I think we all know about good literature: *Without it, we are without . . .*

A Native American colleague said one of the greatest tragedies to befall those who immigrated to this country is that they left the old folks behind. And, in so doing, left the stories. She says that we are always living in a tale, whether we recognize it or not. Cézanne *does* recognize this. She informs us that all our personal histories are part factual, part mythical, and that it is not the "truth" of the story itself that is essential, but what the story produces in the reader.

In *Open Your Heart with Reading,* Cézanne has done us a spiritual service, and this book will be an effective addition to the libraries of educators, parents, and anyone desiring to keep students, children and themselves connected to the joys of literature.

Regie Gibson, Poet

Kurt Vonnegut had this to say about poet Regie Gibson:

> *"When you perform, you are supersonic and in the stratosphere . . . You sing and chant for all of us. Nobody gets left out."*

Gibson is a National Poetry Slam Individual Champion and has been featured numerous times on National Public Radio, on HBO's *Def Poetry Jam,* and on the WGBH-2 program, *Art Close-Up.* His first collection of poems, *Storms Beneath the Skin,* received the Golden Pen Award. He is currently working on two manuscripts and recently completed a MFA in poetry from New England College.

Flights of Fancy

> A great book should leave you with many experiences,
> and slightly exhausted.
> You should live several lives while reading it.
>
> —WILLIAM STYRON

Throughout the course of my life, I've been an explorer, an actor, a murderer, and a priest. I've saved some lives and taken others. I've written bestsellers and I've been illiterate. I've owned châteaux in France and I've begged for bread crusts on the streets of London.

In other words, I've read books.

Fanciful? Perhaps. But maybe fancy is a good—even the best!—entry point into the world of reading. In his lively *How to Read Literature Like a Professor*, Thomas Foster makes, presumably to no one's surprise, the observation that human beings cannot fly. To which I would add, *ah, but we've always dreamed of it*. Long before we aspired to fly to the clouds, much less to the moon, we aspired to simply *fly away*.

Fly away. Leave behind the dreariness and drudgery that oft accompanies our day-to-day lives; leave the illnesses that limit scope and emphasize our weakness; leave the poverty, wars, and cruelty that characterize our species; leave the sure knowledge of our own mortality. Leave it, be somewhere else, be someone else. *Fly away.*

Fly Away

Books make the impossible possible. Frogs become princes; time-travel is ordinary; streets we will never visit seem familiar; people from the past whisper their lost secrets into our minds. Think about it: you have at your fingertips a vehicle that will take you any-where—that will enable you to fly wherever your fancy takes you! You can dream, you can build, you can cry, you can . . . *fly away.* Be whoever you want to be, do whatever you want to do.

It costs nothing but your time and energy. It can be done in nearly any venue. It's legal. It stretches your mind and heart with-out you even being aware that you're growing. Stories carry you outside of yourself, poems touch your soul with a moment of per-fect beauty, nonfiction enlarges your view of the world, plays give you fresh voices.

I have to say something about literature and escapism here—because for those of us who are easily immersed in a book, it's a natural consequence. And it's not necessarily a bad thing.

All good books are alike in that they are truer than if they had really happened and after you are finished reading one you will feel that all that happened to you and afterwards it all belongs to you; the good and the bad, the ecstasy, the remorse.

—ERNEST HEMINGWAY

I've experienced it in both a positive and a negative way. I've been transported and enlightened, taken away from the humdrum of my ordinary life through the magic of words.

And the negative way? When I met my husband, Paul, his two children were four and five years old. Having spent my life up until then carefully choosing to not become a parent, it was something of a shock to suddenly find myself cast in the role of the dreaded Wicked Stepmother.

When I first moved in, a number of factors played into my becoming clinically depressed, aside from a long-standing predisposition to and experience of it. I was dealing with learning the aforementioned role of stepmother, not a relationship for the faint of heart. I had had a major disappointment in my writing career. And I was feeling as though I couldn't write, that I would never, in fact, write again.

How does a rational person respond to these feelings?

I don't know; all I know is what *I* did, and I don't for a moment purport to have been anywhere even in the neighborhood of rational. In the space of two months, I reread the entire Dick Francis opus. Everything he wrote. One book, right after the other—panicking if there wasn't a stack of books beside me. Cringing at the sound of my study door opening, at having to face real life, at being torn away from the very different world of Francis's protagonists who solve puzzles and ride racehorses and (odd, this, when one thinks of it) spend a fair amount of time getting beaten up.

When I finished with Dick Francis, I reached for Michael Crichton.

That's not flying away: it's crawling away, curling up in a metaphorical cave, opting out of life on a semipermanent basis. It's using books as a drug, as alcohol, as any of the escape mechanisms that ultimately bring us more pain than solace.

And it's not what literature and reading do for us, at their best. The dazzling, wonderful, addictive and crucial element of escape is precisely its very lack of permanence: it's an adventure from which one returns.

If we never returned, wouldn't the adventure, some day, turn dull and ordinary as well?

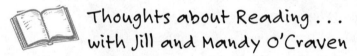

Thoughts about Reading . . . with Jill and Mandy O'Craven

Since this book is starting out with a look at children's literature, I felt it made sense to begin that chapter by asking a couple of real, live children about their reading experiences. So I asked some parents I know to have a chat with their daughters, Jill and Mandy O'Craven of Toronto, Canada.

Jill O'Craven is nine years old and in the fourth grade. She's good at math, spelling bees, singing, and public speaking. Her goal is to someday get rid of cancer. Mandy O'Craven is six years old and in the first grade. She's good at reading and math, loves Webkinz, reading Harry Potter, and playing baseball.

Why do you read?

JILL: I read because it takes me to a world of imagination. It can bring you to a place you would never have been if you hadn't read the book.

MANDY: Because it takes me to a whole different world. I can also meet new friends, and go on great adventures with them.

What is your favorite book?

JILL: I don't have a favorite book. So many books are so good, and so many people have worked very hard on them. They all have a story to tell, and sometimes they are alike but different.

MANDY: Harry Potter, because there are such exciting things happening, and miracles happen too! Like when Harry keeps beating Voldemort, even though Voldemort is really powerful.

What are your favorite kinds of books?

JILL: I do love mysteries and adventure better than all other types.

MANDY: Chapter books that are like Arrow. I like mysteries, adventures, and that kind of stuff. I like books with people who do amazing things.

Why are books/is reading important to you?

JILL: It helps me feel better when I'm upset. And, well, I'm addicted to it. My blood is one percent paper and ink.

MANDY: Because if I'm bored I can always have something to do, and it keeps me happy. Because I love reading!

Why do people tell stories?

JILL: People tell stories as traditions and to explain how things came to be.

Sometimes they're imaginative and sometimes they are serious. Some stories are believable, and some are not so believable.

MANDY: Because they want children to have fun reading them.

Have books/stories taught you about anything about life?

JILL: Never stop reading! But, seriously, I use some techniques from books. Sometimes they teach you things, but not that-important stuff.

You know, like Saddle Club teaches you about horseback riding and horses.

MANDY: It's taught me that reading can help me in life. It would be really hard to live if you didn't know how to read.

What book has inspired you the most?

JILL: I have no idea. They're all good. Not all equally, but some of them.

MANDY: Harry Potter makes me try to do magic all the time. Even at school, I use straws as wands at recess!

Answer the question I didn't ask you.

MANDY: The question is: how long does it take you to read big long chapter books? The answer is, about two weeks for *Harry Potter and the Goblet of Fire* (735 pages)!

ONE

Start at the Beginning

Some day you will be old enough
to start reading fairy tales again.

—C. S. LEWIS

The day is dreary and the children are lonely and bored—sent, as were so many young Londoners during World War Two, to live in the country, a supposedly safer environment than the city. Exploring the house, one of them—Lucy—opens a freestanding closet, pushes aside the clothing hanging there, and steps inside, finding herself immediately in a snowy wood. She's stepped through a boundary between worlds, and is now in a kingdom called Narnia.

We could do worse than begin a book about reading with this episode from C. S. Lewis's *The Lion, the Witch, and the Wardrobe.* The reality is that Lucy's experience is perfectly plausible to children who read (or have stories read to them): our earliest experiences of books have us passing over a similar threshold, going through a door that leads to enchantment.

Let's pause for a moment on that threshold and consider what it is that we're doing.

Liminality is a concept popularized by anthropologist Victor Turner, who explored the threshold concept in terms of rituals and rites of passage. The liminal state of being, according to Turner, is ambiguous, open, and uneasy. Beyond it is entry into community, but only through a process that involves danger, change, and—when the individual is considered vis-à-vis the group—exile.

A child following Lucy into the wardrobe is entering the threshold, the twilight zone of liminality. Here he can explore roles and ways of being, safe in the knowledge that he can still turn around and go back out to the bedroom, to the real world. Liminality does not involve commitment: it is a time of uncertainty and growth, of exploration of identity and formation of values.

Liminality is a place where time stands still: when Lucy returns from Narnia, she is teased mercilessly by her brothers and sister, who argue that she has only been gone for a few moments, not for the hours and hours that she experienced beyond the wardrobe. Liminality is dreamtime and has its own rules, its own reality. Dreamtime is every time, and no time, just as it happens in every place and no place.

That dreamtime is no stranger to children. The most magical of stories have a common beginning: "Once upon a time . . ." The Arabic equivalent of this story introduction is even more telling: "It was and was not so . . ."

The other area where liminality is truly part of the literature of childhood is in its clear delineation of boundaries. In many ways, being a child is all about boundaries: creating them, testing them, exploring them, fighting them. Any parent will attest to the need to set clear limits and stick to them, consistently, at whatever the cost: for a child to feel safe, boundaries must remain firm. They must make sense. Venturing into the boundary area is venturing into unknown territory.

And as they test the existence and pliability of boundaries, children also test their meaning. They already know far more about the power of boundaries than we do: what child will dare step on a crack and risk breaking her mother's back?

Many years ago, I worked in the adolescent psychiatric unit of a hospital—a locked unit often used for forensic hospitalizations: the kids there were very sick indeed. One of them, a slight Cambodian girl, was the only member of her family to have survived a mass killing. Her escape from the images of that massacre was sleep—I can still hear her voice, starting around four o'clock in the afternoon: "Go seepy now?"

The corridor was linoleum in a pattern of black and white squares. Maly took an excruciatingly long time to negotiate the squares, stepping carefully in only the white ones . . . but right on the edge, her feet moving with the concentration and grace of a ballet dancer, of a tightrope walker. Some of the unit staff got impatient, exasperated: "Come *on*, Maly!"

I finally thought I understood what she was doing, though. Watching your family hacked to pieces around you is to live in a world dangerously out of control. Even the tight control of the adolescent unit—every minute scheduled and accounted for, checks by staff every five minutes, being unable to do anything independent—wasn't enough for her. As long as she could step carefully enough, she could control that. That one small thing.

She knew a lot about boundaries, did Maly.

Liminality is an important and heady place to visit, but it's not a place to stay—not unless you plan to live on a locked psychiatric unit. We all have to go back through the wardrobe and into the bedroom, face the separation from our parents, face the horror of the war.

And that's what a lot of children's literature explores.

Tell me a story . . .

It's a refrain that's probably as old as the ages. As soon as children learn the magic of stories—their ability to prolong one's awake time, their ability to keep the shadows and the monsters at bay—they also learn the refrain: "Tell me a story."

So much for theory. Pop quiz: what was your favorite childhood book? Bet you named it, quickly and effortlessly, in the same way you could name your favorite stuffed toy.

I remember mine. It was, in retrospect, a fairly horrible book; why my mother thought it would be appropriate is beyond me, and why I read it over and over, obsessively, even though it gave me nightmares—well, that's beyond me, too. But enough about the pathology of my family of origin . . . the name of my book was *The Tall Book of Make-Believe,* and not only did it have scary stories in it, it had even scarier pictures, including one of a tree with eyes and a predatory expression and another of a child being flattened to drag under a door.

Like it or not, that was "my" first book of any significance. (Oddly enough, it has since then become a collector's item, for reasons that elude me. I no longer had my old copy, but Paul very sweetly searched for it and secured a copy for me—for money that would have absolutely amazed my mother.)

I was determined that my stepchildren would have a better first-book experience than I'd had, and, as luck would have it, I was working as a community relations manager for a bookstore (trying to get a sense of what people read, as a matter of fact) when Paul and I first met.

Of course, I knew nothing about children. My first attempt to engage them in reading went a few steps down my mother's path—I'd fallen in love with Graeme Base's pop-up version of Lewis Carroll's *Jabberwocky,* and proposed making a gift of it. Paul took one look at the pictures, with their swirling colors and sharp teeth and scaled creatures and gently nixed the idea.

Back to the drawing-board.

I'd by then volunteered to do a reading time that we offered in the children's section of the bookshop, and found that my favorite books were ones I could read dramatically—unsure of myself around children, I needed all the help I could get. These books allowed me to get past my child-phobia and really relax into a role.

And that was how I met the Wapiti-Hoo.

> It was Wapiti-Hoo, for I saw him
> Riding a moonbeam ray
> Out towards the mists and shadows
> That hovered about the bay
> Out towards the playful ripples
> Out o'er the waters blue
> And the hills that rise in the misty light
> Sent back his name as he took his flight:
> Wapiti, Wapiti-Hoo!
>
> It was Wapiti-Hoo, for he called me
> While I was watching a star
> Called while the star was telling me
> A message it brought from afar
> Out beyond old Orion
> Where the skies are forever new
> And the words that came when I heard
>   his call
> Echoed afar through the starlit hall,
> Wapiti, Wapiti-Hoo!

It was Wapiti-Hoo, for I know him
He comes to play with me here
Comes in the evening moonlight
When no one else is near,
Skips and leaps in the shadows,
Bathes in the sparkling dew
And he loves me most when I love him best
And says "Good-night" when I go to rest
Wapiti, Wapiti-Hoo!
(Night-Night.)

Wapiti Hoo

Everything I needed to know about children's bedtime picture books, I learned from the Wapiti-Hoo. The rhythm and cadence of the words, the excitement of turning the page, the familiar and beloved chorus, even the final admonition ("Every good children's book," Paul told me once, "ends with, 'and the little boy went to sleep.'")—the Wapiti-Hoo became a fixture in our home every night that the children were with us. Jacob would choose a book for me to read aloud, and Anastasia would choose a book for me to read aloud, and we'd end with *The Wapiti-Hoo*, both children coming in on the chorus with me: "Wapiti, Wapiti-Hooooooooo!"

The book is taken from a poem by John F. Smith, a true Renaissance man who devoted every year of his life to a different field of study (which takes far more discipline than my own wild and volatile range of interests would allow . . . but something I dream of being able to do, someday); it is illustrated by the creative and fanciful Joey Hannaford, who has captured the whimsy and delight of the Wapiti-Hoo. It is also, like many, many excellent books, sadly out of print—but look for it anyway. It can be found, and is well worth the search.

"Long ago and yesterday," reads the introduction, "the Wapiti-Hoo began to play in the velvet night-time, when he feels safest to be his most unusual and wondrous self. The Wapiti-Hoo can fly like a bird, swim like a fish and look like a dinosaur, and can be just about anything he makes up his mind to be! Every part of him is filled with the joy of knowing everything that he knows."

Children aside, I was always struck by that last sentence. *Every part of him is filled with the joy of knowing everything that he knows.*

I think I had forgotten about that kind of joy. You may have forgotten it, too. But Smith knew a great deal about it: the joy of knowledge and understanding for the pure sake of knowledge and understanding. It's why I continued in graduate school long after I was learning anything remotely useful for a career; it's why we sit in bookshops and cafés, difficult nonfiction books propped up in front of us. The joy of knowing.

Not a bad introduction for a child, and not a bad reminder for an adult, either.

In the amazing way that the Universe has of placing things in one's path at the right time, I was working on this chapter when Paul borrowed from the library Richard Feynman's *The Pleasure of Finding Things Out*. Although Feynman professed himself to be a nonreader, his essays are all about the same things that one can discover through books: curiosity about the way things work, about the picture inside the picture, about the meaning of an apparently random structure or situation.

There are many different ways of opening one's heart, many different routes to finding meaning in the everyday, finding joy in discovery. If physics works for you, as it did for Dr. Feynman, you should explore it . . . and art, and singing, and writing: all the titles in the Open Your Heart series speak of finding that meaning through many, often circuitous, routes.

But let's get back to books . . .

Once upon a time . . .

From the beginning, my stepson Jacob was a musician. Not for him were the stories of enchantment, of legends coming to life, of animals anthropomorphizing in the forest. He needed a book that sang, and we found it in Chris Raschka's *Charlie Parker Played Be Bop*. More than a story, this wonderful picture book is like reading jazz aloud: "be bop . . . fisk, fisk . . . lollipop . . . bus stop . . ." Charlie Parker played "no trombone," and the reader is urged to "never leave your cat . . . (turn the page) . . . alone."

Because of Raschka's book, we immediately went down to Harvard Square and bought some Charlie Parker CDs for Jacob to listen to. Because of those two experiences, he elected to take saxophone lessons for many years, until in high school he was finally won over by the glamour of rock and roll.

Have you read books like that? Books that kept you humming, snapping your fingers, tapping your foot? Perhaps part of the magic of so many children's books is in their rhythm . . . in their music. By touching children on so many different levels, books like that allow children to open their hearts with a kind of joy and spontaneity that's a lost art to most adults.

It was and it was not so . . .

Children's books are the doors to enchantment; through them, we get our first glimpses into the lands and creatures that imagination can create.

And just as C. S. Lewis had his fictitious children pass through a wardrobe into a land of magic, so too do we first use books to access that part of ourselves that dreams, that invents, that *sees*.

> So all we could do was to
> Sit, sit, sit, sit.
> And we did not like it,
> Not one little bit.
> And then,
> Something went bump . . .
>
> —DR. THEODOR "SEUSS" GEISEL

Ah. There's the catch—or the rub, as Shakespeare would have it. The bump. The traditional Scottish prayer warns about it: "From ghoulies and ghosties, and long-legged beasties, and things that go bump in the night—good Lord, deliver us!"

Just as the stories that we'll be exploring in the next chapter, stories meant for adults, help describe and share common experiences, so too do children's stories share common children's terrors, and thereby defuse their power.

READING EXERCISE

If you have children in your home, secure one of their books. If not, go to the library or local bookseller and pick up one or two picture books.

Find some time and space to be alone. Don't pick up the books, yet; sit for a moment. Close your eyes. Breathe. Let the magical words float around your brain: *Once upon a time . . . Once upon a time . . .*

Take a deeper breath, one that fills the bottom of your abdomen first and then all the way up. Hold it, and visualize enchantment. Let it go, slowly, and open the book in your lap.

This book is your magic carpet. It's your ticket to adventure. Even if you know this book, open it as though for the first time. Enter into the magic. Read it aloud—not for a child, not for any audience, just for your own pleasure. *Feel* the words on your tongue, in your mouth, on your lips. Say them out loud.

If it feels appropriate, stand up and shout the words (if you're reading *The Wapiti-Hoo,* I sincerely hope that you will shout, gleefully!).

Close the book when you're finished. Hug it to your chest and close your eyes.

Congratulations, you've done it:

You flew away.

Thoughts about Reading . . . with Lady Di

"Lady Di" is well known in Provincetown, Massachusetts. She hosts a weekly show at the local radio station, WOMR, called "Leggs Up and Dancing." She is a justice of the peace who regularly conducts weddings, straight and gay alike. And she hosts benefits for everything from the local soup kitchen to a restoration of the library. She is well known—and well loved. She has worked successfully in a number of responsible professional positions.

I asked her to describe herself. "Gosh . . . it's always hard for me to write anything about myself . . . First, there is always that mystery about Lady Di's voice over the radio . . . is she or isn't she? And until some people get to see me in person, they never know. So I'm going to leave it up to you, as it is a stage name. Lady Di is just a simple person who has an open loving heart who tries to pass on this love through her weekly radio program on WOMR 92.1 FM (womr.org) every Friday night from five to seven pm) and by participating in annual fundraisers to bring love, happiness, and smiles to those who can hear her voice or are able to see her in person so that she is able to give them a hug."

You cannot help but smile, listening to her on the radio or over the Internet. She sprinkles her talk with expressions like, "Sweet Sarah and her petunias!" and "I am unanimous in my decision," and plays the most wonderful music from the fifties and sixties—often singing along in a voice that's occasionally on key. Listen to her some Friday evening: it's a real treat.

And she didn't read—at all—until she was in her fifties.

"I never read as a child," she says; "no one ever read to me. I was dyslexic and didn't know what was wrong with me until I was in my fifties. When I was in third grade, I lost my glasses, and I always blamed my inability to read on that."

She laughs about it now. "I managed to get by. If someone can show me how to do something, then I can do it. That's how I survived as an executive secretary for so many years at Polaroid. I never turned away from anything—I always tried to do things, tried to figure them out even if I couldn't read all the directions, all the material."

Yes, but—she went to medical school, too. How? "I'd manage to read the beginning, middle, and end of something and make some jumps in between."

She finally found out what the problem was. "When I was fifty-one or fifty-two I watched a *20/20* program on dyslexia. That was the first I'd ever heard of it. No one talked about it back when I was a child, and here I was, seeing myself on the TV. It was an awakening, honey."

Times have changed for her. "Now I love reading. I read Patricia Cornwell and I can't put her books down. I stay up all night. I love them. I take them everywhere with me when I travel."

TWO

Storytelling

There have been great societies that did not use the wheel,
but there have been no societies that did not tell stories.

—Ursula K. Le Guin

*O*nce upon a time . . .

. . . There was a young king, part-god and part-mortal, who sat on the throne of Uruk. After a wild and misspent youth, the king becomes fast friends with a wild man named Enkidu who emerges from the forest. But Enkidu is fated to die, and the young king, Gilgamesh, is distraught with grief. He first denies his friend's death, keeping the corpse with him until it rots; then finally he travels to the Underworld to learn important lessons about friendship, mortality and immortality, and life and death.

So goes the *Epic of Gilgamesh*, the first recorded story (written somewhere between 2750 and 2500 BCE) to have survived to our time. It's still studied and read, still touches people, not just because of its age, but because its themes—the anguish of loss and death, the search for understanding—continue to be real and vital problems for people today.

And that is perhaps the first and most important purpose, the *raison d'être*, of storytelling: to help us learn about ourselves and our world, to help us cope with the unknown, and to find comfort in not being alone.

But the *Epic of Gilgamesh* tells us more about the needs of humanity, its hunger for stories, because it gives us other themes that have striking parallels in other cultures and civilizations.

The hero-friendship between Gilgamesh and Enkidu is reflected in the friendship between Achilles and Patrocles, as recorded in Homer's *Iliad*.

The Underworld into which Gilgamesh descends to pursue his friend and gain wisdom can be seen even more vividly in the story of Orpheus and Eurydice, in the *Odyssey*, and in the *Aeneid*.

Powerful women who don't get their way—and make those around them pay for it!—constitute a major theme in stories up into our own time. In the ancient world, we see Ishtar raging out of control in *Gilgamesh*, Medea raging out of control in *Argonautica*, and Juno and Dido raging out of control in the *Aeneid*. Contemporary examples include Meredith Johnson in Michael Crichton's *Disclosure*, the Wicked Witch of the West in *The Wizard of Oz*, the Red Queen in *Through the Looking-Glass*, numerous witches and stepmothers throughout the fairy-tale world, etc.

Interestingly, most of the works featuring powerful harpies were written by men; make of that what you will.

Just like Odysseus after him, Gilgamesh leaves behind his responsibilities as a monarch and goes wandering off on a long, arduous, but ultimately personal quest.

While in the Underworld, he learns of a terrible flood that destroyed nearly all life on earth, one that will never again recur. The Hebrew Bible also tells of a flood, of its only survivors, Noah and his family, and of the promise that no other comparable flood will ever destroy the world again.

The flood story is one worth thinking about. According to one researcher's work, it seems that the list of cultures without a flood myth is nearly nonexistent. Clearly, something happened to the earth at one time, an event so far-reaching and cataclysmic that people on every continent made up stories about it. In the resources section at the back of the book you'll find reference to the study, which recounts flood stories from the Maori of New Zealand to the Inuit and Eskimo of Alaska, from the Ekoi of Nigeria to nearly every First Nations tribe of North, Central, and South America, from Transylvanian gypsies to Arcadians to Samoans to Celtic peoples.

There are other stories present in many different cultures, at many different times, stories that can be grouped (like the flood stories) into various global themes, themes that include:

- creation myths

- hero quests

- heroine quests

- rebirth myths

What are we to make of this? If nothing else, this amazing similarity speaks of *connection:* no man (or people) is, indeed, an island. We are connected by a common mother: Earth. And when things go wrong, they go very wrong indeed—and for everyone. So we find ways to tell of what happened; we try and make sense of the inexplicable. We read meaning into natural events, weave them into a sparkling shining tapestry that tells the story of our family, of our tribe, of our world.

What is that impulse? It's universal; look at any child who has been separated from a parent for a few hours, and note the babbling that ensues when they're reunited. My mother used to say that it took my sister longer to tell us the story of a movie she'd seen than it would have taken to actually watch the movie.

We feel an impulse to share what has happened to us, our thoughts, our ideas. We need to use words to figure things out: how we came to be here, how we fit into the world, what our lives mean.

> Wherever men and women have told stories, all over the world,
> the stories emerging to their imaginations have tended
> to take shape in remarkably similar ways.
>
> —CHRISTOPHER BOOKER

Many authors have done substantial work on the similarities of stories across cultures, and I cannot do more here than point the reader who may be interested in reading more about this phenomenon in their direction. Most of these authors hang their work on Jung's concept of archetypes, "the ancient river beds along which our psychic current naturally flows," and, along with liminality, a really interesting concept if you're trying to interpret your connection to the world and to other people. Along with his thoughts on a collective unconscious, Jung opened new ways of hearing and absorbing the stories that define and connect us.

> The unconscious is like an attic where all the unused or unusable
> material of our personal or tribal experiences is tossed, higgledy-
> piggledy: old wedding photographs, Grandmother's shawl, Great-
> Grandfather's diaries. They pop out of the clutter by accident,
> as when children play there or an inquisitive housemaid
> begins turning over the dusty relics.
>
> —MORRIS WEST

So to start with Jung is to really look at the source of a good many of our interpretations of story, myth, and folktale. Joseph Campbell took it a step further in claiming that most—if not all—stories are related to something he calls a "monomyth," and that individual stories merely present different facets of this one myth (but he also referred beautifully to myths as the "song of the imagination," and so one can forgive him other transgressions!). Bruno Bettelheim takes us back into the world of analysis in *The Uses of Enchantment,* and graduate programs are becoming more and more interdisciplinary, seeing links between mythology and psychology.

> Myths give us story solutions to lessen fear, elicit doses of adrenaline at just the right times, and most importantly for the captured naive self, cut doors into walls which were previously blank.
>
> —CLARISSA PINKOLA ESTÉS

Mircea Eliade talks about myth as "sacred history"—and here's where we really start coming closer to the crux of the matter. There are many people—perhaps you're one of them—who would see that description as a contradiction in terms. Myth is fiction, they would say; history is fact. Yet in the stories that make up our personal and collective histories, in the stories that make up our religions and belief systems, in the stories that make up the ways that we live and perceive ourselves and others, the line between fiction and fact is blurred.

And you have to ask yourself, at the end of the day, whether it's what is important, that distinction. "But does it matter to us after all whether it was a mistaken identity or a wild fantasy?" asks Fyodor Dostoevsky in *The Grand Inquisitor.* "All that matters is that the old man should speak openly of what he has thought in silence for ninety years." Perhaps what matters most to us is what is helpful to our lives. What helps us get through the day.

And for many of us, stories are what do it.

Fairy Tales

Once upon a time . . .

Along with their first cousins, myths and legends, fairy tales are a subset of folklore, a storytelling tradition of a given group of people. Once a story is committed to paper, it leaves the realm of folklore and becomes part of the world's vast library of literature; fairy tales live on the threshold of folklore and literature, a gossamer wing's-breadth apart from either.

> The definition of a fairy-story—what it is, or what it should be—does not, then, depend on any definition or historical account of elf or fairy, but upon the nature of Faërie: the Perilous Realm itself, and the air that blows in that country.
>
> —J. R. R. TOLKIEN

Fairy tales are the light and shadows of our childhoods, the source of nightmares and dreamworlds alike. They are filled with all of the stuff of storytelling: love, dependency, betrayal, innocence, hatred, revenge. They are the cautionary tales of parents and the wildest hopes and aspirations of children; they echo our deepest fears and our eternal desire for happy endings alike.

Fairy tales are where reality and fantasy intersect. How many pouting children wish that their limit-setting parent could go the way of Cinderella's evil stepmother? How many people dream of being awakened—like Sleeping Beauty—by a kiss or a touch, and not need to be sleeping their lives away anymore? How many frustrated parents, in their darkest moments, wonder what it would be like to abandon their children in a metaphorical forest? The story of fairy tales is the story of humanity at its very best . . . and at its very worst.

Which may explain why we have such ambivalent feelings about them.

Tolkien knew the land of Fairie well. He helped populate it by summoning everyone together into one sweeping story: elves and magicians, trolls and fairies, hobbits and dragons alike, and then merging two important storytelling themes—the battle of good versus evil and the tale of a momentous life-changing quest—to draw readers into a world which he made as real as their own.

He is right to speak of an air that blows in that country: we take stories into our hearts very much at our own risk, because if we're not careful, they will touch us, become part of us, change us. I was (and remain) a devotee of Colin Dexter's Chief Inspector Morse, and when Morse died, I wept. My grief was as sharp as if I'd known the man in "real life," because for me—through Dexter's storytelling—Morse was indeed real, was indeed a friend, was indeed someone I would miss terribly.

His (and Her) Story

We all tell our personal histories in different ways, and every time we tell them, the story itself becomes more important than the actual events that transpired. It's not that we lie, not exactly—but perhaps, at the end of the day, our interpretations of events, the meanings that we assign to them, are more important than the actual events themselves.

One of the things I like about author Terry Pratchett is his understanding of stories as they relate to personal histories. Pratchett sees the world as a subjective place—in fact, seems to think that our entire construct of world is subjective—and that it is, in fact, made up of stories.

You build little worlds, little stories, little shells around your mind
and that keeps infinity at bay and allows you to wake up
in the morning without screaming.

—TERRY PRATCHETT

Communications theorist Walter Fisher writes about a comprehensive theory known as the *narrative paradigm,* which claims that people don't organize what they learn as facts in logical relationships but rather retain their everyday information as anecdotal narratives with characters, plots, motivations, and actions. At the end of the day, according to Fisher, all communication is a form of storytelling.

I rather like Fisher's theory. I like thinking of my mind, your mind, as filled with stories, tumbling round and round each other as they might in an electric clothes dryer, and helping us make sense of the world and our experiences in it. And I like to visualize everybody walking around with all these stories inside them, shifting to accommodate new insights, new information, new experiences, constantly reinventing themselves—and us—in the process.

Pratchett takes the story idea a step further: that we filter out much of our experience before it reaches consciousness. We decide what reaches us and what doesn't, and we create constructs that allow us to fit the filtered experiences into our stories.

Humans need fantasy to be human. To be the place where the
falling angel meets the rising ape (. . .) Take the universe and grind
it down to the finest powder and sieve it through with the finest
sieve and then show me one atom of justice, one molecule
of mercy. And yet you act as if there were some sort of
rightness in the universe by which it may be judged.

—TERRY PRATCHETT

So what does all this mean? My sense is that stories are so much a part of the human condition that we tell them automatically, innately, often without even knowing that it's what we're doing. Our stories are inextricably bound up with ourselves, our beings at their deepest and most fundamental level: our stories tell us who we are.

Stories Tell Us Who We Are

Scheherazade

No chapter on storytelling would be complete without a visit to what is known generally (and inaccurately) as the "Arabian Nights"—the *Book of One Thousand and One Nights*. They're actually a collection of stories that have accumulated over thousands of years, with contributions by various storytellers, scholars, and translators; the original was probably written somewhere around 900 BCE.

You'll recognize many of the tales: here is where we meet Sinbad the sailor and his famous seven voyages, Ali Baba and the forty thieves, and Aladdin.

Aladdin's story features a theme that's a favorite in the world of storytelling: the rags-to-riches motif, where a person of lowly birth attains a higher position through trickery of some sort, then experiences a crisis that forces him to become a better person, and finally enjoys success that is the fruit of his newfound maturity. (We keep telling this story, too: consider many films featuring the actor Tom Cruise: *Rainman, Jerry Maguire, Top Gun, A Few Good Men, Cocktail.* Might as well just give them all the same title: *Tom Cruise Grows Up.*) In Aladdin's case, the djinni summoned by the magic lamp Aladdin found gives the boy easy riches, but he obtained the lamp through trickery and that nastiness comes back to haunt him. The sorcerer from whom he stole the lamp comes after Aladdin, who loses all and matures through the despair he feels at his loss. That maturity gives him new strength and he is able to reclaim his lost wife and his money and status.

Sinbad is the Middle Eastern counterpart to Odysseus and other fidgety men who find life at home dull and life on the road (or, rather, on the waves) considerably more exciting. He sets out from Basra in modern Iraq on a number of ill-fated expeditions during which he is shipwrecked (several times), pulled down to the sea bottom, attacked by snakes and rocs, and has other adventures but is rescued each time either through his own cunning or the grace of Allah.

Ali Baba (and I can't help but always visualize him in Maxfield Parrish's painting of the same name) owes his success not to his own devices, or even to Allah's intervention, but to the cleverness of a slave, Morgiana, who seems to extricate him at every turn. Essentially this is a story about taking what does not belong to you: Ali Baba is cutting wood in the forest when he discovers the cave where a group of thieves have left their booty—and overhears the password used to get both in and out of the cave. Ali Baba takes some of the gold he finds and his brother subsequently attempts to find more, though is discovered by the thieves and killed. The thieves come after Ali Baba himself, and Morgiana saves him by killing them all. Hmm. Definitely another theme here . . .

And, then, of course, there's the storyteller herself, Scheherazade.

Imagine Anne Boleyn going to her wedding with Henry VIII of England with her eyes wide open to future events, and you have a sense of what Scheherazade faced. King Shahryar's first wife had been unfaithful; ipso facto, though a singular logic all his own, all wives must be unfaithful. So he took a succession of virgins as queen, killing them on the morning after the wedding so that no other man could have them. Freud would have a field day with this fellow.

Enter Scheherazade, who actually volunteered for the job. She had a plan in place—and she was that most dangerous of creatures, an educated woman. According to Sir Richard Burton, premier translator of the text, she "had perused the books, annals, and legends of preceding Kings, and the stories, examples, and instances of bygone men and things; indeed it was said that she had collected a thousand books of histories relating to antique races and departed rulers. She had perused the works of the poets and knew them by heart; she had studied philosophy and the sciences, arts and accomplishments; she was pleasant and polite, wise and witty, well read and well bred."

And King Shahryar was clearly no match for her.

Scheherazade spends the first evening ostensibly saying goodbye to her sister who, prepared ahead of time, requests a last story, while the king lay awake in the next room, listening. When Scheherazade finished, he asked for another story, but she pointed out that there wasn't enough time, though it really was a pity, you see, because the next story was *even better* than this one . . .

Needless to say, he didn't kill her. Not that morning, and not any morning, as he subsequently spent his nights listening eagerly to one story after another, the words enchanting and dazzling, seductive and instructive, for one thousand and one nights . . . until finally, overcome by her intelligence and creativity (not to mention the three children they'd managed to fit in among the stories), and with a new understanding of the world and of women (*King Shahryar Grows Up*), he makes her queen and they live, one assumes, happily ever after.

Now *that's a story!*

READING EXERCISE

Of course you know all of the "major" fairy tales, many of them, for better or for worse (accurately or inaccurately), thanks to the efforts of the Walt Disney Corporation. But let's try something new.

Set your Internet browser of choice to surlalunefairytales. com and take a moment to peruse some of the stories there. (Those of you who would prefer not to put this book aside in favor of the Internet—and good for you—will want to go to the bookshop or the library and secure a copy either of *The Treasury of Fairy Tales* or *Classic Fairy Tales: Enchanting Stories from Around the World*, where you'll find many of the same stories.)

Skip over the stories that you already know: it's time to challenge your heart. Look for a story that's unfamiliar, that perhaps you've never heard of before. Do you know *East of the Sun and West of the Moon*? What about *Vasilisa the Beautiful*? Are you familiar with *The Twelve Dancing Princesses*? Whatever you do, choose a fairy tale that is new to you in some way.

Fairy tales reveal truths about ourselves. Sit for a moment and breathe deeply. How are you entering into this fairy tale today? Do you want to go deeper into yourself? Or do you want to simply get on the magic carpet it offers and fly away? Either choice is right, as long as it feels right for you, as long as you keep your heart open and see what it is bringing you today.

Now read the tale. When you've finished, sit with it for a moment. Did it surprise you? Make you feel happy or sad? Did it take you away from your world and make another become real to you?

. . . Did you fly away?

 ## Thoughts about Reading . . . with Phil Rickman

Author Phil Rickman was born in Lancashire, though he has spent most of his adult life in Wales and the Border country. He began his writing career as a journalist, eventually switching from print to radio and television, winning awards for BBC news and current affairs reporting in Wales before his first novel—a Welsh political ghost story—was discovered by novelist Alice Thomas Ellis, then fiction editor at Duckworth.

After that came a number of suspense novels through which a sometimes-common cast of characters weave their various stories, and a series of spiritual mysteries featuring Anglican priest and deliverance minister Merrily Watkins.

Phil Rickman still presents programs for BBC Radio Wales, including the book show *Phil the Shelf.* He's also written two novels as Will Kingdom and started a new series under the name Thom Madley—aimed (but not exclusively) at a slighter younger market.

Phil Rickman lives with his wife, Carol, now his most frank and ruthless editor, in a medieval farmhouse on the Welsh border.

Why do you read?

Why do I eat? Why do I breathe?

What book(s) do you remember from childhood?

I remember them all, and some of them influence me still. I'd like to say I'd worked through the complete Proust by age twelve, but sadly I read "kidlit" until I discovered James Bond at eleven.

It was a fairly smooth transition to the (in retrospect slightly insufferable) Bond from Enid Blyton, who wrote about faintly snobbish, private-school educated upper middle-class kids who had amazing adventures in between scoffing buns made by their parents' cooks and fizzy lemonade. The first Enid Blytons had been passed on to me by an older cousin who I think had had them passed on to her, because they were touchingly dated . . . and I fully realized that if I, as a lower middle-class kid from the North country, ever encountered the Famous Five they'd probably pass disdainfully by with their noses in the air. But I still loved those books, and they introduced me to the concept of the literary "family"—a small group of regular characters who reflect different aspects of what's happening. It works just as well with adults.

I particularly loved—and was, I've realized, *strongly* influenced by, a series of Enid Blyton mysteries with titles beginning with R—*The Ring o' Bells Mystery, The Rubadub Mystery.* These were always heavy on atmosphere and sense of place, and they were spookier than anything else she wrote. I was absorbed. I also discovered—again very much period pieces by then but entirely wonderful—the William books of Richmal Crompton and, more contemporary,

Anthony Buckeridge's equally funny Jennings series, about boys at a boarding school—kind of like Harry Potter but where the only fantasy is (where it should be, frankly) inside the characters' heads.

Why are books/is reading important to you?

The honest answer is because it's how I've always made my living. Before getting a novel published I was a journalist. Before that I was a kid who wanted to write novels. I wrote my first at the age of about nine. It was called *The Mystery of Shimmering Cliffs*. I did the illustrations, too, and designed the cover and stapled the whole thing together and my aunts read it and said nice things about it. (Crucial advice to would-be novelists: never show your unpublished manuscript to friends or relations. They will always say how good it is, and you'll never find out how crap you really are.)

What is the function of storytelling?

I don't really know, but I suspect fiction operates on the same level as dreams. You're entering a world over which you have no control. You're a captive. When it's over, you will be unharmed physically but, when you're in the middle of it, it's life or death . . . or more important than that. And the experience is at its most vivid and intense when there's an element of the unexpected.

Now, it has to be said that most adult readers rarely achieve this level of involvement—that is, they no longer *lose themselves* in a book, the way they did as kids. This is because they start to *control the experience,* according to what they think they like. They stick to the same genres and the same authors. They say, *Oh, I hate all crime novels* or *I despise romantic fiction.* These are the people who—to answer part of the next question—are unlikely to have their hearts opened by a novel. It's important, sometimes, to pick up a book you would never normally want to read. If it turns out to be as bad as you feared, you don't have to finish it. But you might just get a life-changing surprise.

How do I know this? Because I present a radio book program in which I interview other authors (over the years I've done everybody from Stephen King to John Updike and the late Joe Heller). Most radio and TV interviewers have not read the book—a producer or researcher skims through it and hands them a list of questions. I *always* read the book. If I like it, it makes for a much richer interview. If I hate it, the author has a bad time, which makes for good radio. It's a win-win situation, especially for me because I'm forced to read books I wouldn't normally pick up with rubber gloves on . . . which sometimes turn out to be amazing.

How can words open one's heart?

Words can open anything: hearts, minds, bank accounts. If the human body is ninety percent water, the mind must be ninety percent words.

Name some authors who have influenced your life/work in some way.

90 percent words

I first earned how to generate excitement from Ian Fleming. His dialogue was generally awful but his action sequences were brilliantly orchestrated. At fifteen, moving on to Len Deighton and the great John le Carré, I decided I wanted to be a spy novelist, but the world, thank God, wasn't ready for a fifteen-year-old spy novelist. In between, however, I was always drawn to mysteries with atmosphere—I loved *The Tiger in the Smoke* by Margery Allingham, a golden-age crime novel, beautifully written and dense with London fog.

There were also, of course, great, imaginative, intoxicating novels which stood alone—like *The Magus* by John Fowles, which I read when I was about eighteen . . . all through the night. I'd probably read it now and spot flaws, but at the time . . . *wow*.

Another suspense writer I discovered was P. M. Hubbard, whose short novels always grew out of their locations. The place was the main character—a village, a remote dwelling, a stretch of coastline, a river—and the human characters were aspects of it. Just how great and how unique P. M. Hubbard was has never been appreciated, and he died in comparative obscurity just around the time I was discovering him, twenty-five years ago. Tragically all his stuff is way out of print. One day . . .

Hubbard also touched—very carefully—on the paranormal, which was where I came in as a writer. I like much of Stephen King and Peter Straub, but in many ways, modern supernatural fiction reached its peak almost where it started, with William Blatty's *The Exorcist*. Much of what followed was fantasy, and I eventually got bored with it. So, after writing four supernatural thriller novels in the 1990s, I decided to start taking the paranormal seriously and deal with what actually happens . . . or does it? Maybe.

Basically, I'm always drawn to atmosphere and resonance, which is why my current favorite crime writer is James Lee Burke, who gives you a full sensory experience. I've never been to Louisiana but, with Jim around, who needs to?

What genre(s) do you read? In what ways does this reading enrich your life?

I read them all because I do a book program. The genre I read most, for pure pleasure, is crime and mystery. Largely because the best writing—the best psychology, the best descriptive writing and the best dialogue—is to be found in this genre. A lot of garbage, too, of course, and the highest garbage level is to be found, unfortunately, among the best-sellers. I could name them, but maybe this isn't the place. The genre I'm least attracted to is probably fantasy, though there are a handful of good ones.

Good novels enrich my own writing; they show me standards to live up to. And if I think I'm writing well, that probably makes me a nicer person to live with and enriches the lives of others. (That's how delusional writers can be.)

Have books/stories helped you form your ideas about life, the world, people, relationships, etc? If so, how?

Quite a few, at different times. For instance, I was inspired to become a journalist by a very funny novel about journalists written by Michael Frayn. It's called *Towards the End of the Morning*, and it's about the kind of people you encounter on a newspaper. I was about seventeen when I read it, and I just wanted to enter that world. Journalists—*real* journalists—are very much a race apart. They instantly understand one another, and they have a way of looking at the world, seeing everything around them in terms of news value. Most of my best friends have been journalists, and I don't think my novels would have worked as well without journalism.

So—bottom line—this slim comic novel is the one that led me in the right direction at the right time. My dad wanted me to be a lawyer . . .

What book has inspired you the most? Why?

It has to be a nonfiction book, *The View Over Atlantis,* by John Michell. It was either the first or second birthday present from my wife. I was a hard-bitten, cynical journalist of 23. A colleague on the paper had read it first and couldn't stop talking about it. Yes, this book changed my life and directed me eventually to what readers tell me is a new genre—the spiritual procedural, as somebody called it.

Essentially, Michell looks at the mysteries in the British landscape and the way people have interacted with the environment over the past four thousand years. It deals with prehistoric sites, sacred places, and folklore. It totally changed the way I looked at my surroundings—now, whenever I go somewhere new, I'm instantly aware of church towers and steeples and how they relate to hilltops and mysterious bumps in the landscape.

John Michell had himself been influenced by Alfred Watkins, of Hereford, who discovered what he called "leys"—straight lines connecting ancient sites. Professional archaeologists thought he was crazy and still do, but they're missing the point. It doesn't matter whether or not leys exist; the *idea* of them leads you into a whole new way of seeing. I was so fascinated that we moved to the Welsh border, where Watkins did most of his research, and that's where most of my books are set. This place is amazing; it just throws ideas at me.

THREE

Faraway Places

The commonplace is defeated here, by I know not
what strangeness. Once across the dunes
we live in an exquisite unreality.

—HAZEL HAWTHORNE

There's a story about Phyllis A. Whitney—which may be completely apocryphal—recounting how she chose venues for
her many novels that were, more often than not, situated in exotic
places. Whitney simply chose a vacation destination, a place she
wanted to visit and, once there, found inspiration enough to make
it the backdrop for her current story.

It's a neat trick that many other authors have adopted—particularly those anxious to write off some of those exotic vacation
getaways in the eyes of tax authorities. But no matter how she got
herself to these places, Whitney did something magical once she
was there: through her words, she transported the rest of us along
with her.

It's a singular gift, this gift of place, and one that's worth thinking about. The concepts of place and space are important; so much
of who we are flows out of the places where we have lived, the

moments of perfect beauty we've absorbed in a special space, the sacredness of one place or another. In my own writing, the place in which a novel or short story transpires can be said, in many ways, to be a separate character itself.

I had to place the conversation with Phil Rickman just before this chapter, for I have never encountered any writing that can make a place take on a character of its own as his can. Places that are meaningless become familiar, nearly sacred, when seen (and expressed) through an author's familiarity and love. I knew nothing about Wales before I picked up (oh, happy chance!) my first Phil Rickman novel; locating it on a map was the best I could manage. Oh, and Cardiff: I'd read O'Neill.

And then I picked up *Candlenight* ("I think if I was writing it now," he wrote to me recently, "I'd be inclined to reduce the final mortality rate quite drastically . . . but, hell, it was a first novel!") and didn't put it down again, reading the entire book through a hot summer night on Cape Cod, unaware of my surroundings as I walked, instead, the streets of Pontmeurig and Y Groes.

The moss itself is a character in *The Man in the Moss,* and the events that happen in *December* are soaked in the history of the area. Read them all, and you'll begin to understand how stories can, sometimes, articulate a place, a space, a geography.

> I found that the wind was rising, bringing with it the soft roar
> of the surf below me. Out on the water white sails plumped
> and power was shut off. A sense of the agelessness
> of sand and ocean possessed me
>
> — PHYLLIS WHITNEY

In my previous book in the Open Your Heart series, *Open Your Heart with Geocaching,* I discussed the Armchair Travel Club. While that's an organized group, armchair travel at its best is random, unexpected, totally disorganized, and delightful. On some very rare occasions I've picked up a book because of its venue—*A Writer's Paris*, for example—but mostly I pick them up because they look interesting.

And then the magic of place seduces me altogether.

I often say that the best writing class I ever experienced was not a writing class at all: it was reading the opus of romance-suspense author Mary Stewart. Like Whitney, she wrote in a genre that is currently out of style. And again, like Whitney, she had a genius for transporting the reader into a venue in such a way that one returned with some effort, as from a long holiday, the sights and the sounds and the smells of that other place still foremost in one's mind. *The Moonspinners* made the countryside of Crete come alive; *Nine Coaches Waiting* did more to explain French culture than any book on cultural etiquette ever could (for a more modern take on French culture, try *Le Divorce*, but I digress).

One of Stewart's masterpieces in this regard is *The Ivy Tree*, which takes place, perhaps prosaically, in the English countryside—but it's an England Stewart knows and loves and communicates so well that I can hear the lambs bleating in the background, can feel the sun kissing my cheeks.

> To the right, the cliff fell sheer away to water, the long reach
> of Crag Lough, now quiet as glass in the sun. To the left,
> the sweeping, magnificent view of the Pennines. Ahead of me,
> ridge after ridge running west, with the Wall cresting each ridge
> like a stallion's mane. There was a sycamore in the gully just
> below me. Some stray current of air rustled its leaves,
> momentarily, with a sound like rain.
>
> —MARY STEWART

England is a theme for poets as well. Who can hear Blake's "Jerusalem," for example, and not have a sense of those "pleasant pastures"?

> And did those feet in ancient times
> Walk upon England's mountains green?
> And was the holy Lamb of God
> In England's pleasant pastures seen?
> And did the Countenance Divine
> Shine forth upon our clouded hills?
> And was Jerusalem builded here
> Among these dark Satanic mills?

Long before I started searching out isolated places to go and write, Yeats had found the same thing at Innisfree:

> And I shall have some peace there,
>   for peace comes dropping slow,
> Dropping from the veils of the morning
>   to where the cricket sings;
> There midnight's all a glimmer,
>   and noon a purple glow,
> And evening full of the linnet's wings.

I, too, have gone off to be where no one else is ("I want to be the only one for miles and miles," as the Dixie Chicks would have it), so was happy to receive an arts residency in a dune shack on Cape Cod, near Provincetown, with its own literary history. I had hopes to meet ghosts in the dunes—Eugene O'Neill, John Reed, Edna St. Vincent Millay, John Dos Passos, Mabel Dodge; they felt as though they were, in some way, "my" people. I was twelve years old in

1968, a watershed year, a year of passion that I lived in my native France, watching the barricades go up, seeing people stand for their beliefs. I did not participate, but it influenced me profoundly—as perhaps only a preadolescent can be influenced!—and later in my reading, I found in those Greenwich Village/Provincetown artists and writers what I always felt to be kindred spirits. The times we live in are not so different: our worlds are both in love with war, in love with profits, in love with power.

So I imagined myself walking those dunes, communing with those spirits; I was again the romantic twelve-year-old, believing in the power of belief. But their ghosts were not there (or, if they were, I could not feel them); my communion, instead, was with the marsh hawk and the tree swallow, with the seal and the whale, with the wind and the sand and the sea. I'd bypassed the interpreters and gone straight to the source, to what fed and inspired those I admired and sought to follow.

And there instead I wrote a story of another adolescent, exiled to a dune shack by anxious parents in 1942, who falls in love unwisely (for what adolescent falls in love well?) and finds herself making decisions about her own beliefs and conviction, influenced in no small way by these same wild surroundings. This story was the dune shack's gift to me, and my gift to that twelve-year-old who still lives inside me, urging me to live significantly, to live on the barricades. I think—I hope!—that the ghosts I sought would be pleased.

Choose Your Vehicle

Any literary genre can fly you away to a place that becomes more real to you, possibly, than your own street. Some adventure novelists are particularly good at it; think of John le Carré, Martin Cruz Smith, even Tom Clancy. Others among them may write brilliantly yet don't give that same sense of the experience of a place: Alistair McLean held my attention, breathtakingly so, but I never felt that I'd *been* any of the places he described.

On the other hand, the late Gavin Lyall was particularly gifted: through him I gained an emotional sense of the Caribbean and a piercingly real feeling of living in rural Finland, where they send a little truck down the runway to clear the reindeer so an airplane can take off. One doesn't easily forget details like that.

Dawn Powell had an incredible gift for allowing the reader to enter into the space she describes. In *Dance Night*, she writes, "These were all busy smells and seemed a six to six smell, a working town's smell, to be exchanged at the last factory whistle for the festival night odors of popcorn, Spearmint chewing gum, barbershop pomades, and the faint smell of far-off damp cloverfields."

You can also choose nonfiction as your vehicle of choice. Travel essays have become an important part of most travelers' trip preparations, and they're great for armchair travelers as well.

Paul Theroux has written some entertaining—and sometimes touching—stories about journeys he's taken. *Dark Star Safari: Overland from Cairo to Cape Town* will tell you more than you ever wanted to know about traveling in Africa. But be sure to also pick up the others: *The Great Railway Bazaar: By Train Through Asia; The Happy Isles of Oceania: Paddling the Pacific; The Old Patagonian Express: By Train Through the Americas; Riding the Iron Rooster: By Train Through China;* and *The Kingdom by the Sea* (his candid and compulsive account of a journey round the coast of Great Britain).

Many readers are no doubt familiar with Peter Mayle's *A Year in Provence* and Francis Mayes's *Under the Tuscan Sun*. Both of these books are well written; both talk about doing things that many of us have dreamed of doing, in places we've dreamed of doing it.

Travel and humor appear to go hand in hand—certainly one needs a certain sense of humor to manage all the problems and lack of control inherent in traveling. The contemporary master of humorous travel writing has to be Bill Bryson, whose work will most decidedly have you laughing out loud, and insisting on reading certain passages out loud as well, both of which may be annoying to those around you. Check out *Notes from a Small Island, I'm a Stranger Here Myself, A Walk in the Woods,* and *In a Sunburned Country* in particular.

Then there are travel anthologies, stories grouped around a theme—difficult travel, women traveling alone, travels where everything-went-wrong-but-we-still-have-a-sense-of-humor-about-it, travels with children and/or pets, gay travel trips and destinations, and so on . . . These anthologies cover a wide range of experiences and have the advantage of bringing different voices to the topic. The stories they contain are relatively short, which in fact makes for great reading when you're actually traveling (all those times you need to stand in line at airports, snatch a few minutes' reading in a hotel or tent at night, and so on), but is also super for getting a whole lot of perspectives in one fell swoop.

And let's not forget travel books themselves. Most people only turn to Lonely Planet or Fodor's when they've already made their reservations, but you can find your heart opened to a whole culture just by reading a book about a far-off destination. I read travel books voraciously. I generally choose a place I'm not likely to go in the near future—the Philippines, say, or Tajikistan—and gaze at the color photographs and read about the customs and try my hand (or, more accurately, lips) at pronouncing some of the travelers' phrases. Talk about flying away!

So try one out. Most bookshops have a travel section, which is great fun to peruse. Generally at either the start or the end of that section is where you'll find the travel essays. See which ones open your heart to becoming a traveler of the mind . . . and maybe even to physical travel as well!

Far-off destination

The Literature of Exile

The route to oblivion is strange and seductive, and that journey, a journey that takes the traveler far from home, is part of the literature of place.

In *The Sheltering Sky*, Paul Bowles—an American expat himself—writes about Port and Kit Moresby, a couple who travel aimlessly through Africa in an attempt to fix their marriage. People do appear to take to the road in order to encounter what is deepest—and sometimes darkest—inside themselves.

> He crawled out of the bed and went to stand in the window.
> The dry desert air was taking on its evening chill, and the
> drums still sounded. The canyon walls were black now,
> the scattered clumps of palms had become invisible.
> There were no lights; the room faced away from the town.
>
> —PAUL BOWLES

The French translation of the song *Guantanamera* as performed by Joe Dassin says, in part: "And the rest of the world is open to me, but I never asked for that much; once I crossed the border, there was nothing left ahead of me." The literature of exile is one that speaks directly to our hearts, that speaks of pain and longing and lost hope.

Keeping the collective memory of the homeland alive is difficult for an individual in exile because of issues such as language, distance, and myriad other problems. Individual authors living in exile often find themselves facing an unfamiliar language, vastly different traditions, and limited economic opportunity. For the most part, they have to contend with an entirely new culture, a different language, and unfamiliar literary traditions. It's not surprising, therefore, that many exiled authors and writers live in isolation and find it difficult to find an audience for their work. Their home culture doesn't understand their experience of exile; their new culture doesn't appreciate the pain and strangeness of vision that they bring to their work.

I just reread the last paragraph and realized how sterile it is. True, yes, but empty nonetheless. I am a child of two cultures and two countries myself, and although I have now lived for most of my life in the United States, there is a part of me that will be forever and completely French. Am I an expatriate Frenchwoman living in America? Or is it when I am in France that I'm the expat? People like me don't know how to answer those questions.

I think it is all a matter of love:
the more you love a memory, the stronger and stranger it is.

—Vladimir Nabokov

But not knowing how to answer the question is a cerebral function, and the problem is that exile has nothing to do with thinking and everything to do with feeling. With longing for a past, for a culture, for a people; Campbell would say for a *tribe*.

I remember the first time I returned to Angers, the city in which I grew up, after a few years spent in the States, and the absolute outrage I felt when I saw the "new" city hall, erected since my departure. How dared they? I hadn't been consulted; I hadn't been apprised. That feeling isn't about returning after moving to another country; that feeling is about the exile everyone experiences from their own past, their own childhood.

> . . . that if we still happen today to leaf through those books
> of another time, it is for no other reason than that they are
> the only calendars we have kept of days that have vanished,
> and we hope to see reflected on their pages the dwellings
> and the ponds which no longer exist.
>
> —MARCEL PROUST

We are all of us, in a sense, exiles; all of us staring back at our pasts with longing and pain. The literature of exile is literature for everyone; its words of loss and desolation speak of our own loss and desolation, and its lessons provide wisdom for us all.

Azar Nafisi's *Reading Lolita in Tehran* weaves a powerful story about the loss one experiences no matter what one's decision—to stay or to go—ends up being. The women who meet at her home on Thursday mornings are already experiencing exile, a disconnection from their hearts and their sexuality. Perhaps, in some sense, one needn't go anywhere to be in exile.

Opening your heart to the literature of exile is opening your heart to longing, to pain, to memory. It is listening to forgotten voices echoing on deserted stretches of sand, snatching at a half-remembered moment in time, longing for something that may not even exist anymore.

Are you brave enough to go there?

Places No One Has Ever Been

The starship *Enterprise* was to "boldly go where no one has gone before," and much of science fiction takes us to those same places: places that exist only in the imagination of a writer but which can become as familiar to us as our own hometowns.

> A little north of the dig, in the sprawling, vaulted Friary, other Green Brothers keep busy in their gardens, busy with their pigs and chickens, busy sky-crawling, busy walking out into grasses to preach to the Hippae perhaps, or to the foxen, who knows?
>
> —SHERRI S. TEPPER

The first science fiction took us to strange places—Jules Verne brought us twenty thousand leagues under the sea, and H. G. Wells posited the invasion of Earth by tentacled Martians. But in the mid-twentieth century, imaginations took off with the first rockets, and writers began to imagine what other worlds might be like.

Which is more difficult to do than most people imagine. Science fiction—good science fiction—really needs to embrace philosophy, logic, and ethics as well to create a world and characters within that world that are all believable. My husband, Paul, explains it best: "Imagine that you're describing a world where iron doesn't exist," he says. "What does that mean? What are the implications? Then consider a world where iron is in scant supply. It changes every-thing—people who have iron would have power, too. You have to think these things through."

Creating a new world is, indeed, a lot of responsibility; the imperative for consistency can be daunting. Religion, politics, geography, forms of government, languages, literacy levels, occupations, and technology are each important considerations. Some authors do it well. Larry Niven's Tales of Known Space series offers a rich set of worlds, where the various cultures all seem to work. Frank Herbert's Dune books even emphasized the importance of the planetary ecology.

Science fiction in some minds (although not all) flows naturally into an allied genre: fantasy. Here, too, worlds are built and populated with their own internal logic, often incredibly painstakingly. The master of world creation, to my mind, is John Ronald Reuel Tolkien. The Lord of the Rings trilogy, combined with *The Silmarillion* and *The Hobbit* describe an entire imagined world, complete with geography, demography, history, and languages . . . ah, yes: the languages. Tolkien had been inventing languages since early childhood, and he repeatedly stated that he'd invented his world for the one purpose of having a setting where his "Elvish languages" could exist. There are a number of other books written about the geography, languages, and peoples of Middle Earth. The search engines are your friends—feel free to explore.

For an example of an author who has gone further than many in making a world come alive and in many ways become real, Patricia C. Wrede, who writes in a world called Lyra, authored an essay, "Perspectives on Early Lyran History: A Monograph" by Kirala Jeseca, ASH (Adept of Sorcerous History), including forty-six footnotes and arguments from opposing scholars on the causality of events and motivations of major historical players. All of it is based on the discovery and examination of a newly released cache of documents. It's a tour de force in creating fantasy literature . . . and a wonderful read as well.

Related to fantasy is another genre called magical realism, a term coined in the late 1920s to describe artists portraying reality in a new way, and adopted by the Guatemalan Miguel Ángel Asturias to describe his poetry and novels when he won the Nobel Prize for literature in 1967. While associated with Latin American writers like Asturias and Gabriel Garcia Márquez, magical realism is truly world literature, stories that are fantastic without using any of the conventional props of fantasy (such as witches and elves). Allende's *The House of the Spirits,* Rushdie's *Midnight's Children,* Kundera's *Immortality,* and Doctorow's *Loon Lake* are all examples of the genre.

And how is magical realism about place? How does it open our hearts?

Because it gives us pause, and it gives us perspective. It allows the reader to look at our own world through the lens of a different world, with all of our assumptions and stereotypes blown to hell and true understanding emerging.

Here's another way of looking at it. David Macaulay wrote and illustrated a fabulous book called *Motel of the Mysteries,* the supposed field journal of a forty-first-century archaeologist uncovering the site of a twentieth-century motel, the Toot'n'C'mon. The archaeologist believes the site to be a sacred tomb: rooms are defined as outer and inner chambers, the DO NOT DISTURB sign evolves into a sacred seal, and the television is—what else?—the Great Altar. I won't even tell you what he makes of the toilet.

Seeing our world through others' eyes can be depressing or invigorating, depending on where we go with the perceptions. That is, at its best, what all of these genres—science fiction, fantasy, and magical realism—do for us as readers: enable us to go somewhere that doesn't exist and look back at our customs, our beliefs, our goals, and our lives, hopefully with enlightened eyes, certainly with different ones.

And who knows, being in that place, at least for the time it takes to read the book, could be the beginning of change, growth, revelation, and happiness . . . in *this* place.

READING EXERCISE

Let's stick with the magical realism theme for this exercise. If possible, try reading one of the books mentioned above before completing this exercise. Now take out a pad and pen—yes, you need to do some writing this time.

Take a moment to quiet your mind. Take some very deep breaths—empty your lungs, all the way down to the bottom, get that last pocket of air out of them. Now breathe in deeply, first filling that same space, the bottom of your lungs, slowly, all the way up. Hold the breath. Think about the breath. Now release it slowly, again visualizing your lungs emptying themselves completely. One more time: long, deep breath in, hold, long deep breath out.

Now imagine someone looking at your life from the outside—from a different culture or a different planet. What are some of your daily tasks that being might find inexplicable? Write them down.

Think about how you dress, the way you greet people, the order in which you do things. Consider for a moment how you wash dishes, make love, tend your garden, relax in the evenings. Try and see them through the eyes of the future archaeologist, or those of a visitor from another planet. Write it all down.

Now look at your list. What seems odd? Which actions could bear several interpretations? How would someone else, looking from the outside, view your life? Would they place the same emphasis on things that you do?

Now close your eyes and do the breathing exercise again. Slowly. Are there things about your daily routine that you want to change based on this exercise? It's not a bad thing, to change perspective from time to time.

Sometimes flying away can involve looking inside, too.

Thoughts about Reading . . . with Anastasia Czarnecki

Anastasia Czarnecki is thirteen years old at this writing, a middle-school student, equitation enthusiast, budding writer, and the author's stepdaughter. She spends her free time either reading or writing, and is often seen walking about the house and bumping into furniture because she has her face in a book she can't put down.

Why do you read?

I read because it is a way for me to forget whatever is going on in my life and enter worlds perfected by authors and characters created for entertainment and enjoyment. I also learn many new words while reading, which I think is good because I like to learn.

What book(s) do you remember from childhood?

I remember reading a book about a hungry cat that was scheming to catch a mouse, but never succeeded. I also remember, in first grade, seeing a book titled *Don't Hurt My Pony* and I really wanted to read it, but our teacher made us do the "five-word check" where we had to go through the first page of the book and count how many words we didn't know, if it was over five, we weren't allowed to read it. I remember that I wanted to read the book so badly that I used the dedication page for the five-word check and when I tried to read it I couldn't understand it at all.

Why are books/is reading important to you?

Books and reading are important to me because reading is a great way to relax and fade into a perfectly interesting world.

Name some authors who have influenced your life/work in some way. How have they influenced you?

Two authors that have influenced me a lot are Libba Bray and Tamora Pierce because their heroines are excellent examples of girl power and that girls can do anything they want to do if they set their minds to it. Whenever I read their work, I'm positive that girls can do *anything*, whether it's as small as saving her sister . . .or as big as saving a hidden world, or showing a whole kingdom that girls can become knights, too.

What genre(s) do you read? Fiction, nonfiction, some of each? In what ways does this reading enrich your life?

I generally read fantasy and realistic fiction. I believe they influence me to think more abstractly and also I believe that reading fantasy has influenced me to use my imagination more than a lot of people I know.

Have books/stories helped you form your ideas about life, the world, people, relationships, etc? If so, how?

Tamora Pierce's *Immortals Quartet* and Alison Hart's *Shadow Horse* have helped me become more concerned about animal rights and care more about the treatment of our faithful companions.

What book has inspired you the most? Why?

I think the book that has inspired me the most is *Young Warriors: Stories of Strength*, an anthology of short stories edited by Tamora Pierce and Josepha Sherman. This book influenced me because it did really show that you can make a difference, even if you are too young to be listened to.

---

n.b. "And what about the Wapiti-Hoo?" I demanded, possibly a little petulantly, when we finished this interview. "Don't you remember the Wapiti-Hoo?"

"Of course I do, Belle-Maman," Anastasia said with all the scorn of her thirteen years. "But it's not like it was IMPORTANT . . ."

Sigh.

FOUR

People

If you can't get rid of the skeleton in your closet,
you'd best teach it to dance.

—George Bernard Shaw

As I write this, several Internet writers' lists are discussing the current literary rage: the memoir. Why is it that we are so attracted to the form?

Perhaps because, in reading about others, we learn about ourselves.

We look to books to tell us how to live—how others live—how we'd never dare live. Sometimes we read to meet people who will comfort us, reassure us, tell us that at the end of the day, all is well. Other times we read to meet people who challenge us, keep us unsettled and uneasy, make us think about our values and beliefs. Sometimes these characters are fictional; other times we meet them through reading history, or biographies, or current events.

All of them can open our hearts.

You're Not in it Alone

Okay. True Confessions. For far too long a time, I was in an abusive relationship.

I have a scar over my right eye even today that reminds me of being slammed into inanimate unmovable objects like walls and doors and kitchen cabinets, but it's my soul that bears the brunt of the hurt, scarred from the emotional abuse that was worse by far than what I suffered physically.

One thing to know about us, about the survivors: we believed ourselves to be completely alone. The shame and the isolation work together to build a wall higher than anyone can ever climb. I may have dreamed of being rescued, but I knew it would never happen.

In the end, I rescued myself, but the scars remained. And, curiously, I seemed to be completely unable to communicate what had happened to me—I, who make my living through words! Another kind of silence was imprisoning me: my inability to articulate my experience in some way that might make it meaningful (if not comprehensible) to others.

And then I picked up a book and saw myself in its pages.

> And later, when I did resist at last, his repertoire was extensive, magisterial: subtle scorn, veiled ridicule, icy silence, absence, presence, absence. He was skilled, a virtuoso, a concert pianist.
>
> —ANITA SHREVE

When Paul and I were dating, I gave him a copy of Anita Shreve's *Strange Fits of Passion*. "Read it," I told him. "Then maybe you'll understand."

Later on, we both read and discussed Anna Quindlen's *Black and Blue*, Jodi Picoult's *Picture Perfect*, and Nancy Price's *Sleeping with the Enemy*, but it is Shreve who best expressed my experience in ways I'd been completely unable to do. She said what I needed to say, and I no longer needed to say it.

I was no longer alone.

> It didn't matter what it was—there were a thousand faults I had. My faults were legion, dizzying. It was because he loved me, he would again say when I asked him why. Because he cared so much. And in the distances my anger would develop (. . .) the anger eroded joy, dissipated a life. It is a fallacy that anger makes you stronger. It is like a tide running out, leaving you depleted.
>
> —ANITA SHREVE

The voices of literature are our voices: they tell others about us, and they tell us about ourselves. Actor Jeremy Northam once said, "All the great novels, all the great films, all the great dramas are fictions that actually tell us the truth about us or about human nature or about human situations without being tied into the minutia of documentary events. Otherwise we might as well just make documentaries." Or, as my friend Daniel Rosenbaum once told me, "Journalists write about fact; novelists write about truth."

And it's comforting at a very basic level to see one's current problems and anxieties mirrored in a story, to watch fictional characters navigate similar sticky situations or deal with similar problems, joys, heartbreaks, grief. In a world that can often be experienced as alienating and isolating, there's comfort in seeing oneself in the pages of a book. Perhaps it's a matter, still, of not feeling alone anymore.

Are you feeling like your family life is a little too dysfunctional for words? Consider those families to which Leo Tolstoy refers as he introduces Anna Karenina: "Happy families are all alike; every unhappy family is unhappy in its own way." Perhaps you're having problems with a parent—read *The Prince of Tides* by Pat Conroy and you'll realize that your father isn't even in the running. A little *schadenfreude* never hurt any!

And Now for Something Completely Different

Sometimes the people we encounter in our reading aren't reflections of ourselves; sometimes they teach us about the kind of individual we'll never be, the sort of person we never *want* to be . . . but the sort of person who fascinates us anyway.

Literary theory calls these people antiheroes, for even as they may play the role of protagonist in a story, they are truly far from being a hero-figure.

The most obvious current protagonist who at first glance should never have become a protagonist is Jeff Lindsay's Dexter, who made his debut in *Darkly Dreaming Dexter;* he's a blood-spatter expert who spends his spare time torturing people. But classic literature abounds with other not-so-nice characters: Melville's obsessed Captain Ahab; Shakespeare's Macbeth, Iago, Shylock, and Hamlet; John Milton's Lucifer. The narrator of Dostoyevsky's *Notes from Underground* isn't someone I'd ever particularly wish to meet, though he serves his literary purpose well: like other writers of his generation, Dostoyevsky was exploring the use of realism in his novels—and what can be more realistic than a protagonist the reader is sure to dislike? Another one of his characters, *Crime and Punishment*'s Raskolnikov, serves a similar function.

A different narrator, Alex in Anthony Burgess's *A Clockwork Orange,* is clear about his role: while he's not against people doing good in the world, he notes that he himself "goes to the other shop." Two of Joseph Heller's creations, Yossarian and Milo in *Catch-22,* are ugly: Yossarian in that he'll do nearly anything to stay alive, Milo in his war profiteering.

And the list could go on and on.

There's something cleansing about these characters. "If the out-law rapes," writes Andre Dubus, "tortures, gratuitously kills, or if he makes children suffer, we hate him with a purity we seldom feel: our hatred has no roots in prejudice, or self-righteousness, but in horror." We enjoy the frisson of horror we feel as we know that it is, for tonight at least, in our lives at least, safely trapped between the covers of a book. And that, perhaps, for our purposes, is really the role of the anti-hero: he (or, more rarely, she) allows us to explore our responses to evil. We may never need to do it in real life, but having experienced it through the lens of fiction, we'll be better equipped to deal with any nasty or unpleasant characters we're forced to deal with out in the world.

After all, when we open our hearts, it's not just to wonder and beauty. To be truly open, we need also to look at the world with clear vision, seeing its flaws along with its magnificence. To embrace life, we must embrace *all* of life. Otherwise we're living in—well, not exactly a fairy tale, since we've already seen how awful they can be, but certainly in a dreamworld. To open your heart is to take in the good and the bad, the beautiful and the ugly, and to sift through it all and take what wisdom you can from it all.

It doesn't mean you have to like it. But you do have to recognize it for what it is, and your reading companions can show you the way. Perhaps they will even inspire you to *do* something about the darker sides of life, about the hunger and pain and violence in the world.

And how frustrating would *that* be for an anti-hero!

How the Light Gets In

"There is a crack in everything," writes poet and musician Leonard Cohen, "that's how the light gets in."

I like that image. Because, to me, it's the truest articulation of the human condition: the light comes in through the imperfections, through the cracks. They're what make us real, alive, interesting. Most of us are neither angels nor devils; we mostly muddle along, generally doing the best that we can, sometimes heroic, sometimes base, messing up sometimes, trying always. Making mistakes ("she needs wide open spaces," sings Natalie Maines, "room to make a big mistake") and trying again.

In one of the other books of the Open Your Heart series, *Open Your Heart with Writing,* author Neil Rosen speaks of finding characters the most interesting when they are outside of their comfort zone, when they behave in ways that are unpredictable; in a sense, he is saying that characters are the *most* true to themselves when they are not behaving like themselves. It's a notion worth thinking about.

The truth, as always, lies in the in-between places.

The Solution to the Problem Isn't Finding What to Call Them; the Solution Is to Stop Thinking of Them as "Them."

Reading does more than teach us about ourselves and about those with whom we cannot identify. It opens doors into worlds we do not know, gives us glimpses of lives that are different than ours . . . and, perhaps, enables us to gain empathy for others, to walk the proverbial mile in their shoes.

I grew up in France, and my first introduction to Americans was through books written by—and about—Americans. Already a budding socialist, I eagerly devoured the parts of American life that were of interest to me . . . the speech of Americans was to me the speech of the people who inhabited the USA of John Dos Passos: labor radicals and advertising executives, sailors and stenographers, interior decorators and movie stars. I read them all, those voices, fascinated by their stories of lives that were so very different from mine. Perhaps the phrase *opposites attract* is truer in literature than it is anywhere else in life: characters whose lives are dramatically different than ours hold no end of fascination for us. Through them, we vicariously experience thoughts we'd never entertain and activities in which we wouldn't engage; we dare, we stretch, we become free . . . we *fly away.*

Read Tony Hillerman's books and you'll find your heart opening up to understanding (as much as a nonnative can) the Navajo and Hopi tribes of the American Southwest. It doesn't matter whether or not you'll ever visit there, or whether you've ever had the opportunity to read or even think about tribal beliefs, practices, and life; reading Hillerman, you can feel yourself to be part of them, somehow, looking out at white people through Navajo eyes . . . and all of it wrapped up in a series of entertaining and often enchanting detective stories.

James Baldwin and Langston Hughes and Richard Wright have filled my head with unfamiliar rhythms, unfamiliar words, unfamiliar experiences, the myriad experiences—that I will never know firsthand—of African Americans. Hughes himself was touched and inspired by the words of others, starting when he was in second grade. "Then it was that books began to happen to me, and I began to believe in nothing but books and the wonderful world in books —where if people suffered, they suffered in beautiful language . . ." he wrote. Influenced by W. E. B. DuBois, Henry Wadsworth Longfellow, and Walt Whitman, Hughes found in himself the voice that was missing from his reading.

America never was America to me.

—LANGSTON HUGHES

Read those words. Read them more than once. Sit with them. There's no way, I think, to read them without being profoundly moved, touched by Hughes's experience in a way that makes it become part of you, too.

From Charles W. Chesnutt I learned of the legacy of hatred of the South through the eyes of the storytellers, far more powerful than its telling in history books or documentaries. Chesnutt looked at prejudice and challenged readers to understand that a search for justice is rewarded when one is white, but punished when one is black. His words resonated in my heart, bringing our times and experiences together as he pointed out how inextricably color differences are braided in with class differences, something about which I had thought rather a lot, and helping me to find common ground with his characters.

And then there are those characters who introduce us to worlds and professions and activities we may never know. I cannot see myself ever becoming a spy, for example, but I have at least a sense of the life from John le Carré and Gavin Lyall and Geoffrey Household. Dick Francis gives us glimpses of life on and around racetracks and racehorses. Phil Rickman allows us into the inner workings and local politics of the Anglican Church. We may not ever want to do any of these things or be part of any of these organizations, but it's nice, in a way, to know someone who does.

And when you read, your circle of such acquaintances and friends just grows and grows. So that, hopefully, we can all get to a point where we don't think of those who are different from us as "them," but really come to see and acknowledge and appreciate, even if not fully understanding, their experiences and their worlds and their beliefs.

READING EXERCISE

What's an experience that's radically different from yours? Do you know much about Muslim men, orphans, opera singers, women in Romania? Go to a bookshop or library and peruse the shelves—either in fiction or nonfiction, as your preferences lead you—and find some people whose lives and experiences and beliefs are very different from yours.

Now read about them. Read actively, asking yourself questions, stopping to ponder an interesting point or two. How would this character respond to a death in the family? What would he or she do if someone bequeathed them a million dollars? How would the character handle a relationship? The more questions you ask, the better you can understand someone whose life experiences and worldview are different from yours.

Maybe if we can all do it—take that leap, manage that understanding—with books, then perhaps we'll be able to do it with real people someday.

 Thoughts about Reading . . . with Andrew Wetmore

Andrew Wetmore is a playwright and software developer living in northern Massachusetts. He has edited newspapers in the US and Canada, and was development officer for the Writers' Federation of Nova Scotia and the founding chairperson of Dramatists' Co-op.

As a reader, Wetmore normally has half a dozen books backlogged on his bedside table, and a couple more stuffed into his backpack. His overdue fines are a significant contribution to the support of the Lowell Public Library.

What book(s) do you remember from childhood?

My Father's Dragon, Weekly Reader books (*The Shy Stegosaurus of Cricket Creek, David and the Phoenix, Follow my Leader, Champion Dog: Prince Tom, TV Humphrey,* the Danny Dunn series), the Rick Brant series (Tom Swift knockoff), *The Golden Egg Book.* My mother read me the A. A. Milne books, and I read them myself, later, many times. There was a book about paleontologist Roy Chapman Andrews that I ran into when I was maybe eight, and that made me think for a long time that I wanted to grow up to dig up bones and ancient cities.

We had a compact, leather-bound set of Kipling that I read right through when I was far too young to appreciate most of what I read. I loved the smell and feel of the books, though, the rhythm of his sentences and the sense of bumping along after his characters on one adventure after another. (Am I the only person in my zip code to have read his first novel, *The Light that Failed?*)

In that same glass-fronted bookshelf we had the 1909 *Encyclopedia Britannica.* I spent long, long afternoons reading here and there in that, beginning with Aachen and then going from volume to volume as the cross-references took me along.

I avidly read the C. S. Lewis Narnia books, and remember that my parents brought me a first edition of one of the set, a gift from novelist Madeleine L'Engle, who worked with my father.

Through my youth and teens I read a *lot* of science fiction. But somewhere around 1968 the output of new works got beyond my ability to keep up, and I pretty much dropped the genre. But I can still quote you whole sections from Roger Zelazny, and list the plot points for almost any Heinlein or Arthur C. Clarke novel.

Why are books/is reading important to you?

John Updike said once that the audience he wrote for was some sixteen-year-old kid wandering through the stacks of his local library. Updike hoped to catch the attention of that reader, and make a connection with him. I'm that reader. In reading I make connections with

Sixteen-year-old kid

so many people that I would be shy to cross the room to talk to, if we were in the same place. In reading I make connections with people long gone, whom I will never meet in this world. And of course by reading I get to experience places and professions far beyond what I will experience in my mere physical life and body.

What is the function of storytelling?

All life is storytelling. It is how we make it possible to embrace or fiddle with the world and the people around us. Hearing the stories of others reminds us that we are not alone, even if the circumstances of the story are nothing like what we have or would want to have in our own lives . . . telling stories to others gives us a chance to delight others by tickling their minds and imaginations.

I know you by the stories you tell, because they show me what excites your mind, your curiosity, your outrage.

I fool you by the stories I tell, for in them I can be a Baron Munchausen of small events, always delivering the telling phrase when it has maximum impact, instead of realizing hours later what I should have said.

John Gardner, the great novelist, teacher, and self-deceiver, said that the task of the storyteller is to offer a vivid and continuous dream to his audience. Experiencing that dream may patch up or shake up a life.

How can words open one's heart?

An opened heart pours out affective and affectionate words; a closed heart speaks in a clenched and cautious way. But I don't know that words in themselves open or bind. On the other hand, without language that is flowing, or that is backing up and building up pressure behind the locked heart's barriers, the heart has trouble knowing itself and what its possibilities may be.

What genre(s) do you read? Fiction, nonfiction, some of each? In what ways does this reading enrich your life?

I enjoy novels that have plots and characters, rather than the sort of post-narrative text that is sometimes so stylish. Trollope, Dickens, Patrick O'Brian, Margaret Atwood, Eric Kraft, David Daniels (murder mysteries set in my hometown, so I walk the very streets, etc.), Jane Austen, Donald Westlake, Linda Barnes, J. I. M. Stewart, Mary Renault.

I read exploratory history of the Barbara Tuchman style; biographies of people I feel I should know more about.

I read plays (Alan Ayckbourn, Michael Frayn, Shakespeare) with a tactical eye, partly enjoying the text and partly looking for how I would stage it.

I read widely, but not too deeply, in that fascinating library category: *New Fiction*. I bring home bags of books, dive in and read until the book lets me down. If it doesn't, of course, I finish it. But I see no point in letting an author torture the reader with crimes of grammar and character inconsistency and shallow thought.

What book has inspired you the most? Why?

The authors of the Bible give me words that give me hope. Battle scenes, sexy poetry, cooking recipes, land surveying, and pointers to the meaning of life: who could want more?

Answer the question you think I should have asked you.

I am too tired and lazy to do most of the things that I would like to do, and that I recognize as important. Reading engages me in adventures and quests I would never otherwise be able to manage . . . but on my own time. The text does not know that I devour it a few pages at a time, in bed after work or early in the morning: it accepts me and speaks to me whenever I can make myself ready for it.

FIVE

It Was the Best of Times

It is from numberless diverse acts of courage
and belief that human history is shaped.
Each time a man stands up for an ideal,
or acts to improve the lot of others,
or strikes out against injustice,
he sends forth a tiny ripple of hope.

—Robert F. Kennedy

When I'm putting together a list of my five or ten favorite books—an excruciating task that, surprisingly, presents results that have changed little over the years—the novel that consistently comes in at first or second place is Pauline Gedge's *The Eagle and the Raven*.

It's a long (but not long enough—I could have happily read on and on and on) historical novel set in early Britain just at the end of the Roman conquest. The reader sees the occupation through the eyes of Caradoc, one of the last chieftains to surrender—an occupation of stealth, of softness, of luxury rather than of battle—and then later from the point of view of Boudicca, another warrior chieftain. It explores their different decisions—Caradoc lives out his days in luxurious imprisonment in Rome, while Boudicca kills herself in the forest of her home—and the ways that people view freedom and oppression.

But that wasn't what opened my heart. What opened my heart was the feeling of mists rising in the mornings along the river. It was the twitch of fear I felt when Caradoc was out in the forest too late and felt the Raven of Panic at his back. It was the fact that I cried at the final words—"in the west, the light of freedom flickered and went out."

Pauline Gedge was the first author to whom I wrote a "fan" letter, telling her how much I loved this book. I've written to many authors since then—having later discovered myself how isolating writing can be, and the delight of hearing back from readers—but I'm not sure that any was as heartfelt as that first letter.

Robert Kennedy spoke of a "small ripple of hope" that is sent out when someone stands up against injustice. Reading *The Eagle and the Raven*, I felt more, not less, in touch with my own times and the injustices visited on people in them. If fictional characters tell us ultimately about ourselves, then characters living in historical times can do so as well.

The past is a doorway. It's a doorway that leads us back into our family tree; that helps us know where we came from. And novelists and nonfiction writers alike are perhaps the best guides through that doorway.

Do storytellers make good historians, or is it that historians are particularly good storytellers?

Historical fiction is a review of the world. Either what could have been, what was, or maybe, according to the author, what should have been. I think what it can do is educate people in a way that other genres cannot for the simple fact that they are necessarily part of a place and time that many of the readers may not be entirely familiar with. This education is further expounded upon by the patterns of more critical thinking that may historical novels require. When readers dig into Harry Turtledove, for example, and he is rewriting a section of how the world may have been, the reader can't afford to watch passively; the book will pass him by. The reader is far more engaged in the implications of historical fiction. It may be that no one is making a grand statement about the possibility of a world where Nazis rule, but even more subtle information about the character of a well-known historical figure. Even this kind of minute information, like a revelation about the bigotry of a figure like Christopher Columbus can be enlightening to people in a way that no other genre can. Historical fiction has the ability to rewrite what people take for granted as a reality of the world. We celebrate Columbus because of his great contributions—people take for granted that he must have been a good man as well and a real "hero" in the epic sense of the word.

—NIKKI FOSTER

Historical fiction and historical narrative alike are touchstones: they are the way that we connect to our past, to our present, even to our future.

Even people who think they have no interest in the past can be lured into reading about it by a good storyteller. Consider, for example, this brief excerpt from David von Drehle's *Triangle*, one of many books written about the horrors of a fire that devastated a New York sweatshop in 1911: "Late summer was a season of dust and grime. Half the metropolis, it seemed, was under construction, competing skyscrapers racing toward the clouds, a third and then a fourth bridge stretching across the East River. The hot, damp air was full of dirt, cement powder, sawdust, and exhaust from the steam shovels."

Or this opening line of the first chapter in *Between Silk and Cyanide*, Leo Mark's account of code-breaking during the Second World War: "In January 1942 I was escorted to the war by my parents in case I couldn't find it or met with an accident on the way."

Can you really resist reading on?

History is our genealogy, the genealogy of humanity. We might know that Uncle Ernie was a black sheep and that Great-Grandfather had facial deformities—but we want to learn about them, anyway: they're part of our story, part of who we are, their blood moving in our veins, their smiles and flat feet and mannerisms showing up in our own mirrors. Is the history of humanity any different?

In My Hometown . . .

I find myself drawn both to place and to history; they seem inextricably entwined. When I moved to Manchester, New Hampshire, once the site of the largest textile mill complex in the world, I was naturally interested in the history of the Amoskeag Mills. But in a way, I had already read about them—many years ago, I lived in another mill city: Lowell, Massachusetts, and there I read Nancy Zaroulis's *Call the Darkness Light*.

It's possibly not the best writing around, but the story is compelling: set in Lowell during the two decades before the Civil War, the novel tells the story of Sabra Palfrey, a Lowell "mill girl," who with her sister weavers and spinners was part of the first generation of American women to earn her own money and make her own living, apart from the demands of husband and family; the novel deals with the social conflicts that arose from this departure from the rules of the past. It also includes a fascinating cast of characters, including Utopian dreamers, Shakers and Millenarians, abolitionists, and the deluge of immigrants from Europe who came to where, they were told, the streets were paved with gold.

Reading the history of a place where you live—whether via fiction or nonfiction—is an amazing experience. After reading Zaroulis's novel, combined with some nonfiction books such as Bruce Watson's *Bread and Roses,* I was unable to walk through the downtown streets of Lowell without hearing the echoes of that time: the excruciating loud sound of the looms, the heat in the summer when windows couldn't be opened for fear of contaminating the textiles, the cruelly long working hours . . . and, on the other hand, the ability for a woman to be paid for her labors, to finally have some money that is clearly her own. Those echoes have followed me to Manchester, where daily I walk through streets that were "owned" by the Amoskeag Manufacturing Company, once the largest textile producer in the world. Those streets are alive with the ghosts of mill workers, strikers, union activists, and mill owners—but I cannot imagine how empty they would be if I were not a reader. Can you?

It's not a bad way to open your heart to your own environment. Do you share your daily walks with ghosts from your city or town's past? Have you read old accounts of your community? Visit your local historical association for manuscripts and a reading list, and find something there that attracts you. Read what you can, and think about what you've read when you're out and about. Every place has a history, some of them enormously interesting and compelling.

I don't think you'll see anything in quite the same way again.

The other place I live is Provincetown, Massachusetts, and it has just as rich a history as Manchester—a history that is even more interesting to a writer, perhaps, as it has long been the site of an artists' colony, begun by Mabel Dodge and boasting such luminaries as Tennessee Williams, Eugene O'Neill, Edna St. Vincent Millay, and present-day "stars" Norman Mailer and Mary Oliver. But the seafaring side of Provincetown is just as interesting, as noted in the following op-ed piece I wrote that appeared in the *Cape Cod Times:*

The race times were very close: a scant two minutes between the first and second finishers once the 40-mile course was done. The Rose Dorothea's victory would have been sweet under any circumstances. The fact, however, that the schooner had lost her top foremast when rounding Gloucester's Eastern Point made the win something for the record books, and the awarding of the coveted Fisherman's Trophy—the world's largest sailing prize—an achievement to be proud of for generations.

And perhaps just a small reflection of that pride and excitement was felt by some of us present in the library last Friday afternoon as the Rose Dorothea's winning cup was installed in its new home. There was no official ceremony: no ritual words were spoken, no speeches made, no fanfare accompanied the action; only a few quick photographs, a few curious smiles, a few disinterested glances.

So where did the excitement come from?

It's not about the race itself: that took place too long ago to be meaningful to most people. And it's not about the Rose Dorothea herself: we're all very familiar with her appearance as we work and read around her model on the second and third floors of the library. And it's not just because the cup itself is exquisitely beautiful: the town itself is filled with beauty, from the galleries on Commercial Street to the sunsets at Herring Cove.

Perhaps, though, there is some unspoken understanding that at some level the cup serves as a metaphor for Provincetown itself: a juxtaposition of the old (and some would say irrelevant) with the new. The beauty of the past, shining and polished and restored, sitting in the midst of the present . . . and of the future. Provincetown is, after all, a place of change, of layers, of metamorphosis. From the Mashpees to the colonial settlers usurping their lands; from the Portuguese fishermen to the displacement of Greenwich Village, as hip young artists and writers "discovered" the same qualities that keep drawing people here, to the tip of the Cape, which in many ways might be the very tip of the world . . .

Because people are not here by accident. Provincetown is a place where people come, many of them very deliberately, to find something: peace, a home, inspiration, a living. And what could be a better representation of that place than a working Grand Banks schooner that, crippled and against all odds, won a race that we scarcely remember today? How can that schooner be better remembered than through something so big, so gorgeous, so frankly over the top that it defies us forgetting what it's about?

And what better way for the town to show the connection between the new and the old than to have it in the library, which was the Heritage Museum, which was the Methodist Episcopal church, which was . . .

You get my drift.

There will be a formal occasion to welcome the Fisherman's Cup to its new home. There will be proper words spoken and polite applause. But for me, the real installation happened last Friday, with only a few of us looking on while another piece of Provincetown was unobtrusively fitted into place.

I grew up in Angers, France, and it's worth noting to American readers that history feels very close to people in Europe—closer, perhaps, than to people who live in a newer country that was never invaded. I remember being at the weekly open-air market and seeing someone's sleeve pushed back, and the tattooed identification number on her arm becoming visible. My sister and I played on a half-buried concrete structure across the street from our house—a bunker used by the Germans occupying Angers to direct submarine activity off the coastal cities of Nantes and Brest. So that when it came time to study the Second World War in history classes, there was a part of me that already knew. And continuing to read about it out of interest filled in more blanks.

Is it so very odd that, now, much of my own fiction takes place during that time?

What if . . .?

We cannot talk about history without talking about what might have been, a whole subgenre known as speculative fiction (a term coined by Robert A. Heinlein) or alternate/alternative history, which takes a known historical event or period and postulates a different outcome.

It's by no means a new genre: there are examples of speculative fiction in antiquity (Livy wondering what would have happened if Alexander the Great had attacked Rome), in the nineteenth century (a short story by Nathanial Hawthorne contemplates a perception that people from the past are still alive in 1845), and of course in the twentieth century (H. G. Wells's *Men Like Gods* brings in an element of time travel that will become increasingly popular in speculative fiction throughout the century, although the most famous time-travel novel had already appeared—Mark Twain's *A Connecticut Yankee in King Arthur's Court*).

Want to try it out? It's not for the faint of heart, but Neal Stephenson's *Cryptonomicon* is an excellent example of speculative fiction that you might want to consider. It's also a great exercise for flexing your own creative muscles: take a major event from world history and ask yourself how our lives would have been changed had the event been different. The easiest way to start is, unfortunately, with wars: what would the world be like if the United States were still under British rule? If the Nazis had won the Second World War? If John Kennedy hadn't been killed when he was?

You're limited only by your imagination.

Historical Fiction

This is definitely a "best of times/worst of times" proposition. There's been some very good historical fiction written—see my obsession with Caradoc and Boudicca at the beginning of this chapter. But there's also a lot of writing out there that concerns itself very little with historical accuracy and makes my teeth hurt. One reason I don't even like the History Channel—such wasted potential, with most of the programs poorly written, often not well documented, and of a sensationalist tone. But I digress.

One way to access the past is, of course, to read books written in that period. But another way of entering into the experience is through a story told by a modern writer about a past time, allowing the reader to engage with the characters, the plot, and the time, all at once.

At its best, historical fiction provides a connection to the past. If the writer is making some kind of effort to employ accurate history as a plot tool, that "full circle" effect can be achieved. It's a truism that history repeats itself, and perhaps there *is* something to be learned by the mistakes made in the past. Or plausible alternate endings can be used to show how other decisions could have affected our lives today. It offers us the chance to ask ourselves why we are where we are, and how we may—or may not—have gotten here.

My colleague Kathy Page puts it a little differently. "Reading historical fiction can do that only if the authors are willing to get their facts straight, assuming what they are reading is at least reasonably correct in the first place. There is nothing more jarring than any media that presents history with blatant errors in it. It's depressing to know that the vast majority of the public will swallow it whole, assuming the misguided mantra, 'if I saw it on TV, it must be real.' Twice as bad if the writers say they went to any amount of trouble to attempt accuracy."

"If in doubt," says Page, "list it as historical fantasy, please! I can suspend my disbelief better that way."

Bored? Find some well-researched and well-written historical fiction and let it be your vehicle in which to fly away . . .

READING EXERCISE

Pick a time. Any time.

Now find a book or a story that deals with that time. Challenge yourself: if you don't know anything about ancient Egypt, this is a good time to learn something. If the Napoleonic Wars were a little fuzzy in history class, try them again. Or pick up something on the Russian Revolution or Guadalcanal or Cortes. All I ask is that it be about a person or a period you aren't already familiar with.

Write down what you think you know about your chosen person or time. Tuck it away somewhere, and set aside a good space of leisure time to read the book you've chosen—vacations are a good time for this, when you don't have a thousand details about work and daily living crowding your mind.

Now just relax and read . . .

Read with energy, read with intention. Your mission is to learn everything that you can. Ask yourself questions as you go along; ask the author questions as you go along; ask the characters questions as you go along. Treat your reading as a dialogue, not a lecture.

When you've finished, sit with your book closed in your lap. Breathe deeply. Close your eyes, and summon an image of the place(s) in which the book took place, the characters you learned about, the customs of the time. See them all again, as vividly as you can, in your mind.

Open your eyes. Without thinking much about it, articulate (out loud or on paper—your choice) the central theme or idea or knowledge that you've taken from this book.

Now look at the assumptions you'd written before you started reading. Were any of them true? Which ones? Which ones were far off the mark? What do you know now that you didn't before you began reading?

Extra credit: In the coming weeks, try and use your new knowledge somehow. Talk to others about the book you read, or about something interesting you learned, or about one of the characters who did or said something that's stayed with you.

We can always fly away to the past. We just need to know where to look for it.

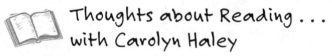

Thoughts about Reading . . . with Carolyn Haley

Carolyn is a dedicated word nerd whose life revolves around letters and images on paper. A Yankee by birth, she migrated from southern New England to rural Vermont, where she now lives with her husband (who's as into metal as she is into paper) and, like him, works at home with critters for neighbors and a view out every window. She has been writing professionally for ten years, editing professionally for more than twenty years—and reading every day since she was about four. She is the author of *Open Your Heart with Gardens*, another book in the series to which this book belongs. A colleague put together a Latin phrase that sums up her passion: "Lego, ergo sum:" I read, therefore I am.

Why do you read?

I can't *not* read!

I read because I am lonely and curious and meditative. Reading assuages all three.

What book(s) do you remember from childhood?

The Black Stallion; At the Back of the North Wind; everything written by Mary Stewart; many horse and Indian stories; some poetry collections; Dr. Seuss.

Why are books/is reading important to you?

Reading allows me to both connect and unplug. To learn and to imagine. Because I do not read tragedy, horror, or anything "dark," reading enables me to maintain hope and understand other people and walks of life, to visit other places and times. It also teaches me how things work and allows me to figure out how many things integrate. Through reading I can communicate with people I will otherwise never meet but wish I knew. And also communicate with people of like mind.

What is the function of storytelling?

To convey—whether it be a moral or a lesson, or just to entertain and stimulate ideas.

How can words open one's heart?

By choosing to read and remember words that mean something to you. Simplest way is to memorize or post a quote that really rings a bell inside you.

Name some authors who have influenced your life/work in some way. How have they influenced you?

Dick Francis, Barbara Michaels, Mary Stewart all influenced my desire to write and style of novel-writing. Though I am not a prodigious writer, my novels are extremely important to me, and through writing them I am challenged in a positive way and get to know myself and other people better. Writing novels also gives a kinship with other writers whose work I read.

What genre(s) do you read? Fiction, nonfiction, some of each? In what ways does this reading enrich your life?

I read mostly fiction except when desiring to learn about specific subjects. Then I seek out books on those topics. In fiction, I read mystery and romantic suspense, especially series; some fantasy and science fiction; occasional historical and general.

Have books/stories helped you form your ideas about life, the world, people, relationships, etc? If so, how?

Books have definitely formed a lot of my ideas about life by feeding my interests, answering my questions, and challenging my philosophy.

Is there anything you'd like to add?

I read in order to write. Other people's words-thoughts-concepts-syntax stoke my mental furnace, enabling me to process and output my own ideas. I don't think I could write if I didn't read, for my brain requires the mechanical tools of language in order to engage its creative engine.

Writing, like all arts, involves both emotion and craft. One without the other falls flat. I find that I often can't harness one without the other. So without the steady fuel of reading, I don't get enough mental energy and discipline to write.

There's also a comfort quotient. When my mind is disordered (especially when I want or need to write and it's coming hard), I find that reading quiets my emotions and helps my brain sort itself out while I'm following somebody else's narrative and inventing visual to go with the words. In both these respects, reading is therapeutic. Which is why I read as much as I can!

SIX

The Butler Did It

Without mysteries, life would be very dull indeed.
What would be left to strive for if everything were known?

—CHARLES DE LINT

I t's been said that there are only seven (or three, or name-your-number) true plots and that everything ever written is derivative from one of them. That's like saying there's one way to be human: you're born, you live, you die, and anything else is derivative.

How Many Plots?

Aristotle may have been the first author to discuss plot, though the concept was in existence well before he wrote about it. In *Poetics*, he argues that stories must have "a beginning, a middle, and an end." Sounds like a plot to me.

He didn't stop there: it is Aristotle who first articulated two "types" of plot-driven stories. Aristotle called them tragedies and comedies; we know them by the more familiar "happy endings" and—well, *not* happy endings. And they do different things indeed to one's heart.

Others have focused in smaller brushstrokes than Aristotle, and the number of people weighing in on the topic is surprisingly high.

We have Norman Friedman (drawing on prior work by R. S. Crane) in 1955 establishing what he saw as the major plots:

Fortune Plots, including:

- Action Plot: Classic all-action sequential story.

- Pathetic Plot: Weak character loses out.

- Tragic Plot: Failure of a strong character.

- Punitive Plot: Bad guy gets just desserts.

- Sentimental Plot: Weak character wins through.

- Admiration Plot: Ordinary person wins through.

Character Plots, including:

- Maturing Plot: Person goes through life transition.

- Reform Plot: Fallen person restores their position.

- Testing Plot: Noble character is tested to the extreme.

- Degeneration Plot: Attractive character falls from grace.

Thought Plots, including:

- Education Plot: Protagonist learns something important.

- Revelation Plot: Ignorance is abolished as truth is revealed.

- Affective Plot: Tension between thoughts and feelings.

- Disillusionment Plot: Loss of ideals and consequent effects.

But we needn't stop there. Foster-Harris, drawing on and expanding Aristotle, speaks of three fundamental plots:

- **Type A:** Happy ending: Foster-Harris argues that the "Type A" pattern results when the central character (which he calls the "Initial" character) makes a sacrifice (a decision that seems logically "wrong") for the sake of another.

- **Type B:** Unhappy ending: this pattern follows when the "Initial" character does what seems logically "right" and thus fails to make the needed sacrifice.

- **Type C:** Literary plot, "in which, no matter whether we start from the happy or the unhappy fork, proceeding backwards we arrive inevitably at the question, where we stop to wail." The literary (or, some would suggest, postmodern) plot is activated by fate, not decision. The critical event takes place at the beginning of the story (instead of at the end, as we see in both happen ending and unhappy ending stories), and the rest of the story has an inevitable feel to it.

A British literary analyst, Colin Jackson, asserts that "there are only three stories proven to engage an audience. I choose to name them hubris, discardation and new order." An example of hubris (pride that will be punished) is Michael Crichton's *Jurassic Park*. An example of discardation (loss) can be seen in the movie *E. T.* And, finally, an example of the new order plot (change) is the film trilogy *Star Wars*.

Rudyard Kipling once said that there are sixty-nine plots, but as he didn't bother to specify what they are, it's hard to take his assertion too seriously. French literary critic Georges Polti comes in second in the numbers: he said that there are "exactly 36 dramatic situations . . . and therein we have all the savor of existence." Both men lived in the nineteenth century, a time perhaps of excess and overstatement.

Irish playwright Denis Johnston originally argued there were seven core plots in the theatre but added an eighth to include the Indiana Jones film plots.

Kurt Vonnegut in an acceptance speech at an awards ceremony in New York City spoke at length about plots. He first suggested that a writer can get away with just one story. "If you stayed at home tonight and watched TV you would see the same story over and over again," he explained. "I call it man-in-hole. But it needn't be about a man or a hole, just somebody who gets into trouble, gets out of it again. People love that story."

But Vonnegut thought a second structure offered possibilities: "I call it boy-meets-girl. But it needn't be about a boy or a girl. There is somebody on a day like any other, expecting absolutely nothing, who comes across something perfectly wonderful. Loses it. Gets it back again."

So . . . there are *two* core plots? Well . . . maybe. But then there's Hamlet, without a standard structure and brings neither good nor bad news. Vonnegut's conclusion? "So I've just proved to you that Shakespeare is as poor a storyteller as any quackydoodle!"

Australian sociologist John Carroll argued in his book *The Western Dreaming* that "Western culture runs on stories . . . without the deep structure of archetypal story, a life has no meaning." He identified nine core themes: the virtuous whore; the troubled hero; salvation by a god; soul-mate love; the parent; the value of work; fate; the origin of evil; and self-sacrifice.

What Is the Point of Plot?

Thinking about plots seems to be the realm of a few specialized individuals: writers (trying desperately to get one), literary critics (bent on taking said writers' works apart), academics (to describe a cultural phenomenon), and psychiatrists (to tell us what the plots say about us).

Carl Jung suggested that certain images belonging to what he called a collective unconscious may be wired into the human brain, causing us to respond favorably whenever we encounter them. His theory of "archetypes" says that characters such as the earth mother, the foxy trickster, the dark menace, and the heroic warrior, who pop up in the mythology and literature of every culture, are embedded in a "racial unconscious" shared by all human beings.

Joseph Campbell, anthropologist and mythologist, added that humans also respond instinctively to an archetypal storyline, something he called *The Hero's Journey*. An individual is called on a quest, meets a mentor and various allies on the road, fights enemies before confronting the ultimate evil, goes through a symbolic death and resurrection, and eventually brings back some sort of elixir or magic bullet to save the tribe.

Anything New Under the Sun?

As important to some authors as plots are themes. It can be argued that many if not most of Neal Stephenson's books are about money. Michael Crichton writes about science, whether it's the soft science of anthropology in *Congo* or the hard science of design in *The Andromeda Strain*.

Is there such a thing as a "new" plot? Probably not. Even Tolkien freely admitted taking plot points from Beowulf . . . but he went on to make those plots his own. And that's the crux of the argument: maybe everything is old, but every new author, if he or she is accomplished enough, makes it new. Just because I loved *Romeo and Juliet* doesn't mean I'm going to dislike *West Side Story*, after all!

So . . . *Did* the Butler Do It?

We certainly can't talk about plots without talking about mysteries, the royal family of plot-based stories. The last twenty years have seen a trend in mysteries toward character development in addition to—and sometimes, some would argue, in place of—plot, but the plot remains the fulcrum of the mystery.

Mysteries come in many guises, from the hard-boiled and hard-bitten stories of Dashiell Hammett, Mickey Spillane, and Raymond Chandler to the "cozies" that include recipes for shortbread and feature protagonists who run bed-and-breakfasts. And, of course, everything in between.

The first mystery writer was, arguably, Edgar Allan Poe. He's certainly seen as the father of modern mystery, for whom the Edgars—mystery fiction's awards—are named. *The Murders in the Rue Morgue* introduced Auguste Dupin, possibly the first fictional detective. In true mysterious fashion, Poe's death continues to be a subject of fascination and speculation (suicide? rabies? alcoholism?).

Police procedurals have remained a perennial favorite with mystery readers. Professional detectives—whether in the employ of the police or other governmental agencies, or as private investigators—can dazzle the reader with their expertise and ability to draw conclusions from evidence, interrogate suspects, and solve puzzles. For no death in any of these books is ordinary or obvious.

Most of my favorites are English. There's something singularly comforting about an English country house murder mystery. Talk about happy endings!

Catherine Aird's books about Inspector Sloan, CID department head in West Calleshire, England, are a good place to begin. Sloan is an intelligent man saddled with the twin problems of a sergeant whose only talent and aspiration is to drive fast cars fast, and a superintendent constantly taking adult-education courses that influence his take on every case.

(Sloan's problems with his boss are not his alone: far across the world in Four Corners, New Mexico, Tribal Police officer Jim Chee of the Navajo Nation has a similar problem—a supervisor with little imagination and even less tolerance for it in others. It's a problem with which many people seem to resonate.)

But back to English procedurals. P. D. James brings us Adam Dalgliesh, occasionally angst-ridden, a published and well-known poet, who rises in rank at the Metropolitan Police as the series advances.

Colin Dexter's Chief Inspector Morse, intelligent, irascible, and extremely fond of the more than occasional alcoholic refreshment, has already been mentioned in this book: yes, at the end of the series, Morse dies. But it's a long and wonderful journey to get there, and after reading all the books, one has the impression that one knows Oxford rather well. There is even—God bless capitalists—a tour you can now go on of "Morse's Oxford."

Ian Rankin takes us to Scotland, a cold and often violent view of Glasgow in particular, but with such a flavor for the place and the characters that you want to read on.

Two Americans, Elizabeth George and Deborah Crombie, write extremely English mysteries. Deborah Crombie's protagonists are Scotland Yard Superintendent Duncan Kincaid and Sergeant Gemma Jones; Elizabeth George brings us Detective Inspector Thomas Lynley and Sergeant Barbara Havers. And how is it that I'm able to reel all those names off as though I knew them? Because I do. And this is part of the attraction of this sort of book: it allows you to meet people, people who are often as real (if not more so) than your landlady or the person who works in the cubicle next to yours. I look at the class tension between Lynley and Havers—and the sexual tension between Kincaid and Jones—and these are feelings I've experienced, feelings with which I can identify. Probably you can, as well . . . which is part of what makes it a great read.

And once we've finished with police procedurals, it's only a short step to private detectives. The first and most recognizable of these sleuths is, of course, Sherlock Holmes, but Americans soon took over the genre. Too many murders appeared to be taking place in genteel drawing rooms, and Raymond Chandler decided to put them back in the streets: in the 1930s he wrote an essay in the *Atlantic Monthly* that defined a whole genre, the hard-boiled detective novel, which included a wisecracking detective, the extensive use of metaphors ("He looked at me like an entomologist looking at a beetle"), uncluttered writing, and a familiarity with the mean streets of a Gotham-like metropolis. If you only read one book from this genre, read *The Long Good-bye* and you'll see where a generation of crime novelists got their material.

Ross Macdonald, another classic hard-boiled detective novelist, uses the past to explain his killers' motivations. That psychological thread is present in Georges Simenon's Maigret books, as well; Maigret is less action-oriented than some of the other police investigators, and he shares Morse's preoccupation with himself. The series as a whole, though, presents something of a psychological tour de force. Ed McBain also wrote procedurals with a definite psychological slant.

Sherlock

Nancy Pearl in *Book Lust* has pointed out that the 1990s saw a slew of women invading the field, both as authors and protagonists, making the genre a little less hard-boiled but still not close to the tea cozy: Sara Paretsky, Linda Barnes, Sandra Scoppettone, S. J. Rozen, Sue Grafton, Janet Evanovich (if a reluctant bounty hunter can be included in a list of private detectives), Marcia Mueller, and Karen Kijewski . . . as well as the many that I've neglected to list. You get the drift.

The ladies are not alone. One of my favorite authors, Dennis Lehane, has a wonderful series involving two private detectives who work out of a church tower in Dorchester, Massachusetts, and use their lifetime knowledge of Boston and its people to investigate crimes.

Amateur detectives feature in a number of popular mysteries; they're often people who are plunged unexpectedly into a dramatically difficult situation and need to extricate themselves or a loved one—and, in so doing, solve the mystery. Harlan Coben's Myron Bolitar, for example, is a sports agent who lives (rather endearingly) in his parents' basement and conducts investigations related to his clients in the sports world. He definitely has Chandler's wisecracking down pat!

Here, in no particular order, are the occupations of some of the genre's amateur detectives: Little old lady (Agatha Christie), psychologist (Stephen White, Jonathan Kellerman), priest (G. K. Chesterton), monk (Ellis Peters), nun (Veronica Blake), rabbi (Harry Kemelman), lawyer (John Mortimer, Laura Caldwell, and a slew of others), caterer (Diane Mott Davidson), newspaper reporter (employed, Jan Burke; unemployed, Laura Lippman), professor (Edmund Crispin, Amanda Cross, and others), and of course, everyone's favorite dilettante and man-about-town, Lord Peter Wimsey, brought to us by the inimitable Dorothy L. Sayers. The latter is popular enough to have an Internet list devoted to the discussion of things related to mysteries and to Dorothy-L (as the list is named) in particular; another list features a monthly reading and discussion of each of her Lord Peter books.

Essentially, with the popularity of the genre still exploding as of this writing, there are few professions that cannot (and do not) form the backbone of a series in which a person may be called upon to conduct investigations and solve crimes.

Many people feel that character-driven mysteries are doing the genre a disservice. Keep the character for the literary novels, they say, and let's see a humming good plot here. Amaze me with its labyrinthine twists; dazzle me with the tricks of the illusionist; *tell me a story*. That's how I fly away.

At the heart of this disagreement—which is more important, plot or character?—is the real issue: is life that easily divided? Which is more important, food or water? We all want to see life as a series of absolutes, of either/or questions, of clear decisions. I like this; I don't like that. She's bad; he's good. Soccer is better than American football. And so on.

That would make for a very orderly world, granted. And a thoroughly uninteresting one. Most importantly, however, regardless of its attractiveness or lack thereof, it's not the world in which we live.

We live in an uneasy world, one in which bad decisions are made for good reasons—and vice-versa. A world where good does not always triumph over evil. A world where the "right" way to go or the "right" thing to do is rarely clear . . . and the notion of right itself must be delimited by quotation marks. A world where people make mistakes, pick themselves up, try again . . . and fail again. A world where the options and issues are never binary—and yet people try to impose some sort of binary categorization on them in a futile bid at control and understanding. Mostly control.

And it's a world of texture. A world where the whole is greater than the sum of its parts, where complexity rules, where people are a combination of wonder and horror and everything in between. That's the world we live in, and that's the world that writers have been called to describe, to illustrate, to explain.

So in a sense what I've done here is something very artificial: separating out the issue of plot from the organic whole of the novel. Forgive me. I'm as eager to stay in my safe comfort zone as the next person!

Ahem . . . So . . . Did He Do It?

I can't talk about dinner without discussing dessert. Chocolate (especially dark Belgian chocolate) is my life. Well, that and really good coffee, also best enjoyed in a postprandial moment of relaxation. But I digress.

Just as I can't talk abut a meal without talking about dessert, I certainly can't talk about plot without mentioning the mother of all plot devices, the surprise ending.

Of course, every mystery author will tell you that his or her book has a wonderful twist at the end. Many do. Others seem a little half-hearted about the whole enterprise.

My current favorite in the twist-ending sweepstakes is Dennis Lehane's wonderful *Shutter Island*. No, of course I won't give it away. What I will say is that when I finished the book I took a deep breath and went back and opened to the first page again. I had to read it over again, immediately, to see how he did it.

That's a surprise ending.

The real king of the twisted ending, however, at least in contemporary literature, has to be Thomas H. Cook, in both *The Chatham School Affair* and more especially in *Breakheart Hill*. Cook writes brilliantly and both of these books are extraordinary in many ways.

I tip my hat (no mere metaphor, that—check out my photograph in the back of this book!) to all those who can keep us guessing up to the last minutes: Jack Williamson in *Darker Than You Think*; Terry Pratchett in *Thud!* and *Strata* (the latter, come to think of it, gives what is essentially a surprise ending on every page); John Irving in *A Prayer for Owen Meany*; Rafael Sabatini in *Captain Blood*, Mary Stewart in *The Ivy Tree*; Ole Edvart Rolvaag in *Giants in the Earth*; Graham Greene in *Brighton Rock* (a nasty ending, that one); Chuck Palahniuk in *Invisible Monsters*; Jeffrey Archer in *Twelve Red Herrings*; and Ambrose Bierce in *An Occurrence at Owl Creek Bridge*.

Also we need to acknowledge the short stories of Guy de Maupassant, O. Henry (bet you'd forgotten *The Gift of the Magi!*), Rudyard Kipling (in particular *The Pit That They Digged*), Saki, and Damon Runyon. There's also a surprise ending to Tad Williams's fantasy trilogy *Memory, Sorrow, Thorn* . . . and, if I stick to stories but move away from books for a moment, it seems to me that every episode of *Twilight Zone* had a wonderfully twisted ending. Harlan Ellison's *A Boy and His Dog* fits the category. And "this isn't a surprise ending," writes my colleague Mark Wise, "but *The Tangled Lands* by Will Shetterly is definitely twisty. It's a prequel to *Cats Have No Lord*. The darned thing nearly gave me cerebral whiplash!"

I was talking about twisted endings with a number of my colleagues, and one of them, Odile Sullivan-Tarazi, pointed out that looking further back still is relevant: "For their original audiences," she writes, "several of the extant Greek tragedies offered surprises within the development of the story as well: Medea, murdering her own children and then escaping like a god; Philoctetes, who increasingly seems less and less likely to leave the island with Odysseus and Neoptolemus, so that, when he finally does (as the audience would have expected from the beginning), after a false ending to the play seems underway, it has the effect of a double surprise; Oedipus, who not only leaves the city, rather than continuing to rule on (as he does in the version recounted in the Odyssey), but who blinds himself as well."

And how does surprise open our hearts? It keeps our minds agile and our feelings young. As long as I can be surprised, there's hope—for me, for the world, for my perceptions of everything around me. It's when things become too predictable that gloom sets in.

So let's stay surprised. Let's stay agile. Pick one of these books or find one of these short stories and settle in to be taken in by the most seductive of companions: the master storyteller.

READING EXERCISE

The plot is the epitome of "tell me a story." You've had the opportunity to think about a lot of different plot devices, twists, and turns throughout this chapter: now it's your turn.

Tell me a story.

Start with something simple: you're at a seaside town, walking out on the fishing pier. The day is sunny but windy. There's the taste and smell of salt in the air. You're just thinking what a beautiful day it is, when suddenly . . .

Complete that thought.

 Thoughts about Reading . . .
with Elizabeth Chadwick

Author Elizabeth Chadwick has been addicted to stories ever since hearing her first one at her mother's knee. She grew up around books and when not reading stories, was making them up. Elizabeth began writing tales of medieval historical adventure and romance in her teens but it wasn't until her thirties that she was taken on by a publisher. Her first published novel *The Wild Hunt* won a Betty Trask Award, which was presented to her at Whitehall by HRH Prince Charles. Since then she has written another sixteen books and has been short-listed four times for the Romantic Novelists' Association Major Award in the UK. Whether reading them or writing them, she remains addicted to books. Read more about her at elizabethchadwick.com.

Why do you read?

I read fiction purely and simply for the purpose of being entertained, although I often learn something along the way, which is a bonus, not an expectation.

What book(s) do you remember from childhood?

Myths, legends, ghost stories. I sucked them all up. I was especially fond as an older child of Homer's *Iliad, Odyssey,* and (Virgil's) *Aeneid.* I loved collections of folktales from around the world—the Bunyip, the Baba Yaga, how Rabbit stole the fire. *Aesop's Fables* was another favorite. The Arthurian cycles, Robin Hood. I loved horsey books too. I read all the Mary O'Hara novels and the Elyne Mitchell's Silver Brumby books. I wasn't so keen on tame pony stories though. I thought they were a bit boring! *Green Smoke* by Rosemary Manning, *Worzel Gummidge* by Barbara Euphan Todd, the William books of Richmal Crompton, *Heidi* by Johanna Spyri, *The Wind in the Willows, Winnie the Pooh.* I read loads of boys' comics such as *Eagle* and *Hotspur,* which were passed on from the boy next door.

I read factual books on horse breeds, dog breeds, nature books, wild bird and butterfly identifiers, histories of the American West, encyclopedias. I was pretty voracious.

Why are books/is reading important to you?

It's a relaxation, an entertainment, an invitation to visit worlds other than one's own and become absorbed in them. Books feed and stretch the imagination.

What is the function of storytelling?

Well I use it myself as a form of entertainment, but I guess it's a way of educating, and of filtering society's expectations and norms—as well as desires. It's also a way of playing "what if" from a safe distance. One can try out different roles by becoming involved in characters and scenarios where one might not want to go, or which might not be possible in real life.

Name some authors who have influenced your life/work in some way. How have they influenced you?

Dorothy Dunnett—for showing me how to play with words and

explore the richness and texture of language. For the depth and scope of her research and her characters. I remain in awe.

Roberta Gellis—for showing me that it was possible to write romance novels that were historically accurate and thumping good stories at the same time.

Cecelia Holland—for showing me that as long as you breathe life into your characters, it doesn't matter what culture or age group they are, readers will relate to them. I am thinking of her Mongol warrior Psin in *Until the Sun Falls*. He's fifty years old, a hardened warrior who's risen under Ghenghis Khan's rule. When I read the book I was in my twenties and working in a shop. My life couldn't have been more different and yet I identified with Psin in every way when I was reading that book. I really wanted to drink kumiss, dwell in a yurt, and live out on the Steppes!

What genre(s) do you read? Fiction, nonfiction, some of each? In what ways does this reading enrich your life?

I read across the board. All genres of fiction are grist to the mill. I have to have variety and couldn't stick to just one type of story. For example, to list my most recent reads: *New Moon* by Stephenie Meyer (teenage high school werewolves and vampires), *Old Scores* by Bernardine Kennedy (gritty UK relationship novel), *The Water Devil* by Judith Merkle Riley (fourteenth-century historical with plenty of humor), *The Whale Rider* by Witi Ihimaera (young adult, slightly mystical story of a Maori girl). I'm totally eclectic. It's a bit like the shout line for Windows: "Where do you want to go today?" In nonfiction I generally read research for my own writing, so it's all either academic or primary source medieval material.

Have books/stories helped you form your ideas about life, the world, people, relationships, etc?

I have never really thought about it. I suppose they must but it's by a process of instinct and osmosis—rather like a child being fed. You eat the food and don't actually realize you are growing, but one day you can reach the door handle. It's honestly not something I consciously think about. Books do, greatly enhance one's general knowledge and broaden one's scope but I don't consciously form an opinion of something because "the book said so." I always question . . . and then have to and look it up in another book!

What book has inspired you the most? Why?

Many books have inspired me down the years and I don't think there is a "most" book. However I cite *Hanta Yo* by Ruth Beebe Hill as one of the all time greats. It's the story of a tribe of Lakota Sioux on the eve of the coming of the white man. It's a profound, moving, deeply spiritual novel about the life of the Lakota. It's also a great story and about lives lived a totally different way to my own. It certainly made me think about things after I'd put it down.

I do think people should be free to read what they want and what suits their lifestyles and personalities. So often I see references in the press to people "reading trashy novels" and this annoys me. One person's trash is another person's treasure house and comfort. As long as people are enjoying what they read and getting something from it, does it matter?

SEVEN

Everything I Know About Life I Learned from a Novel

But I don't want comfort. I want God, I want poetry. I want real danger, I want freedom. I want goodness, I want sin.

—ALDOUS HUXLEY

From Whence Wisdom?

Wisdom comes to us in the most unexpected places.

Not from owls, certainly. The myth of the wise old owl (A. A. Milne notwithstanding) is just that; I was shattered to learn that the real bird is actually quite thin and quite stupid. So much for another cherished belief.

But some of the most unexpected books and stories bring us wisdom.

My husband, Paul, became libertarian after reading Robert A. Heinlein's books, reading about people taking responsibility for their own actions (of course, Heinlein was also misogynist, and Paul happily did not follow him down that road!). In *The Moon Is a Harsh Mistress,* when characters were writing a new constitution for the moon, it was suggested that anyone who wished to become president should be automatically excluded from the running.

I think that's a brilliant idea.

I was raised in a family where there was money—significant money—but with that money, we were taught, came responsibility. We were constantly made aware of those who had less than we did, and of our obligation to help them. Later, as my own values started to take shape as separate from those of my family of origin, and I worked out my own sense of obligation to the community around me, I did what many others do: I made connections with those who believed as I did. I worked among them, had friendships with them, conducted my love affairs within the parameters of people who thought the same way that I did.

It's a lovely way to live, really. It provides a sweet and gentle cushion between you and the realities of a world that rarely behaves the way that you want it to. It's also wholly artificial and impossible to maintain, an illusion—but what twenty-year-old doesn't fall in love with illusion and want to make it last for as long as possible?

Even before politics and world events intruded on my own sheltered environment, books led the way. From them I learned about capitalism and greed, ideas that were foreign to the fragile world I'd constructed around myself.

"Things are in confusion," the Devil's voice boomed out, "and believe me, the confusion will get worse! That's the kind of time when a man of cool wits can make his fortune!"

"I have no interest in fortunes," Gustav said, then compressed his lips. Perhaps he protested too heartily.

"Yes, of course," the Devil said, throwing his arms out left and right, not in a mood to haggle phrasings. "But I'll tell you this: it's a wonderful moment for SOMEbody. If not you, then somebody else."

—JOHN GARDNER

And perhaps that is a gift, too, albeit an uneasy one: reading makes us look *away* from the mirror as much as it forces us to look into it. It makes us consider those who think differently than we do, those who act in ways we find incomprehensible, those who anger and sadden and shame us.

It's not bad training, all in all, for Real Life.

Why Not?

Adventure. We all like the sound of it, but it's often accompanied by awkward situations, uncomfortable lodgings, food made from parts of the animal you didn't know existed, and a distressing sense of yourself as being very small, very insignificant, and ultimately very narrow and limited in the "great Scheme of Things."

Books can help you travel and experience adventure vicariously, of course. But once in a while, they can prod you toward the real thing.

Art Buchwald was living in Paris at about the same time I was. I was nine years old, the daughter of a very unhappy American mother who read Buchwald's columns voraciously and always wondered if she might run into him at the American Church in Paris (which was, actually, in Neuilly, where most of the Americans we knew lived as well). In one of his columns, now happily in print again through the anthology *Americans in Paris* by Adam Gopnik, Buchwald recounts that he moved to Paris on a whim. "Unlike many of my friends who came to paint the world's greatest picture or write the great American novel, or others who came to escape nagging parents, unhappy love affairs, and suburban boredom, I actually had no reason for making the trip."

You have to think about that for a moment. To go somewhere, not just to visit, but to live, and to do it entirely on a whim—that takes self-confidence! *Quel homme!* Where do we find the courage to do that sort of thing—to step out of the ordinary, the expected, the preordained? How do we get the idea that it can be done . . . and that we could do it? Reading Buchwald's words makes me want to. It really does.

Going Out on a Limb

Adventure may not be something you look for: sometimes it finds you, That was Deborah Rodriguez's experience when, in the wake of the September 11 tragedy, she volunteered to go help rebuild Afghanistan. Surrounded by nurses, teachers, doctors, and social workers, at first she was embarrassed to admit to her profession— hairdresser; she wasn't anyone's idea of an aid worker, with her spiky red hair and long fingernails and cigarette habit. But, as she reports in her wonderful book *Kabul Beauty School,* she soon found that she had brought a gift to the cloistered women of Afghanistan that was unequalled: the gift of economic freedom. Now the school is flourishing (and Rodriguez has herself married an Afghani man), with an impressive mission statement: "The mission of the Kabul Beauty School and Oasis Salon is to provide nonliterate as well as literate women in Afghanistan with access to a comprehensive vocational training program that teaches both the art and commerce of beauty."

Not a bad life-lesson for the rest of us to get from a book.

Rodriguez didn't know what she was doing; she brought some skills and some education and a big heart to the table. Books like this challenge; they make us want to do more, want to *be* more. They make us ask ourselves the difficult questions and spend time trying to find the answers.

And that's a lot of what opening your heart is all about.

These are modern examples, although many more can be found in the Western canon, in the authors that make up the literary curriculum of many colleges. These worthies have been occasionally, since the 1990s, referred to as the DWEM—Dead White European Males—but still bring a great deal of our past and our present together, and the intelligent reader will take what she can from the curriculum and supplement it as needed. There is something for everyone to learn from the works of Chaucer, Dante, Cervantes, Dickens, Goethe, Montaigne, Voltaire, Tolstoy, and Shakespeare. Harold Bloom in particular has argued for the canon; to read, according to Bloom, is to first become a "common reader" as celebrated by Samuel Johnson, who wrote, "for by the common sense of readers, uncorrupted by literary prejudices (. . .) must be finally decided all claim to poetical honors."

Poet Helen Vendler is another person who believes in memorizing important literature; she herself had memorized many of Shakespeare's sonnets by the time she was fifteen. But the memorization only has meaning if we make it have meaning; if we carry the words as a companion through our lives, to lean upon in times of sorrow and to be inspired by in times of exhilaration and decision. Ultimately it is what we do with what we have read that gives meaning to the words, no matter who wrote them.

Coming to Grips

Death. We avoid even thinking about it, using euphemisms to speak of people "passing," as though even *saying* the word would touch us, cast an evil eye on us, make us vulnerable.

Yet death is what awaits us all, death is what *frightens* us all. And words can help us come to grips with it.

Poetry is the first and most direct means of access, at least to my mind. Edna St. Vincent Millay's "Conscientious Objector," with its strength and resolve: "I shall die, but that is all I shall do for death." Randall Jarrell with his eloquence about the life—and death—of pilots in wartime; one wonders, in the end, which was more futile. "When I died," he writes in "The Death of the Ball Turret Gunner," "they washed me out of the turret with a hose."

> In bombers named for girls, we burned
> The cities we had learned about in school—
> Till our lives wore out; our bodies lay among
> The people we had killed and never seen.
>
> —Randall Jarrell [1]

It's not just the senselessness of war that we can read about. Poe's central conflict in "The Raven" was his grief over the death of his beloved Lenore. Robert Burns recounted "A Mother's Lament for the Death of Her Son." John Donne, Walt Whitman, Mark Twain, Christina Rossetti, Willa Cather all wrote about death, daring us to look at death, challenging us to be touched with grief.

In *The Book Thief*, Markus Zusak speaks with the voice of Death itself to describe horrors of Nazi Germany. Jodi Picoult's *The Pact* deals with one of the most difficult deaths imaginable—the suicide of a teenager. (Teen suicide is, of course, a new phenomenon in neither literature nor life: Shakespeare already wrote one of the more definitive examples in *Romeo and Juliet*, mixing the intensity of both love and death with the intensity of adolescence in a toxic but immensely beautiful formula.) But while we're on the subject, suicide is another popular theme with authors from Tolstoy to Goethe, from Etgar Keret to Sylvia Plath . . . again, what we see here is the struggle to articulate the unknown, the endless fascination with what frightens us, and the only way we're able to cope: by trying to see it from as many perspectives as we can.

When my stepdaughter Anastasia was still in kindergarten, the father of one of her friends died. Paul and I felt that it was important for her to go to the funeral, to experience a death that was not close to her, to start the process of thinking about death before it came to live in her heart. And at its best, that's what death in literature does for us: allows us to experience grief, anger, mourning, pain . . . and learn what it will be like when real death, real grief, real mourning comes to live in our hearts.

It's all made more difficult because death has replaced sex as the taboo of our times, so we cannot talk about it. It is something we cannot experience—yet—but only imagine, so we cannot understand it. That ignorance and that silence combine powerfully to build fear inside us, and it can be only countered by sharing the imaginative conclusions of others, by breaking the silence and facing the fear. And words—novels, short stories, poetry, memoirs—are what can do that best.

Elizabeth Bronfen and Sarah Webster Goodwin write that "much of what we call culture comes together around the collective response to death," and literature, as we have seen, is the ultimate expression of culture, its signature line. From books we can see how others face death, grief, and mourning, and we can experience it vicariously through characters with whom we identify. Through them, we can start to articulate our own understanding of death, our own beliefs about it, make our own decisions about our own deaths, and begin to understand our own needs around loss and grief.

In others words . . . learn about death, and in the process, learn about life.

Taking it Easy

One of my favorite scenes in all of literature is that of Mole coming out of his hole on that first really fine day of spring in Kenneth Grahame's *The Wind in the Willows*. I love that moment: I can feel the sun on my face and hear the insects buzzing and smell the heady explosion of scent, and sense that, nearby, is the river and Rat and adventure. But before all that is the simplicity, the sheer physical joy of that moment of warmth after the cold and darkness of the winter.

I've learned a great deal about simplicity—and made my own commitment to it—since then: from Henri Nouwen, from Henry David Thoreau, from reading about Mennonite and Quaker cultures. I've learned about civil disobedience from Thoreau (again) and Martin Luther King. I've read all the books that teach all the things that eventually we accept, come to call our own . . . or reject and move in another direction. But none of those life-lessons can top this one, about slowing down and staying in the moment: the sensuality, the sheer pleasure of that instant, Mole's delight in coming up into a world of warmth and light.

Some stories are best told as . . . stories.

Other People's Lives

In the chapter about people we talked about how we can explore lives different from our own through literature. It's worth being reminded of now: Ralph Ellison's *Invisible Man* talks about the experience of being of another color; *All Creatures Great and Small* gives us a glimpse into a country veterinarian's life. *Walden* encourages us to take a simpler, more deliberate approach to our lives. Thornton Wilder and Tennessee Williams allow us to be voyeurs via the theatre, eavesdropping on intricate and deadly family secrets.

The list can go on and on, and what are we to make of it? That we learn about people by listening in, shamelessly, on their conversations; by observing their environments, their friendships, their responses to events; by thinking about their issues and decisions.

We can meet them all through literature, and learn from them so that when we put the book down, when we leave the theatre, we still have something of them burning inside of us.

They help give us our wings.

READING EXERCISE

Think of your favorite book. Quickly, without thinking about it. Have it?

Now consider the characters in that book. Did they face difficult situations? Do they dare to think and consider and do things that you've never thought or considered or done?

Could you?

Maybe not those same things, but there's a reason why you remember this book, why it's so close to your heart. What is it that you're taking from it with you? How does it enrich you, make you stretch, make you dare?

Try and think about those qualities, sometimes. And look for others in every book you read. This is your schoolroom, and your teachers are the wide, amazing array of characters who are happy to be with you anytime you want them there.

Not bad teachers. Not bad friends. Not a bad way to learn and grow and . . . fly.

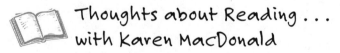

Thoughts about Reading . . .
with Karen MacDonald

Karen MacDonald is the Library Operations Director at the Provincetown Public Library in Provincetown, Massachusetts. When asked for a biography, she wrote, "Karen MacDonald enjoys a life of Sense (teacher, librarian, nonfiction writer . . .) vs. Sensibility (singer, artist, poet, daydreamer, Cape Codder . . .) As a child, nobody understood her except books." That does say it all!

It actually did feel like magic when I suddenly realized I could read! (The book was entitled *I Made a Line*. "I made a line go up and down/I made a line go all around . . .") Sometimes the book itself, unopened, gave off a strange power. There was a hardcover collection of fairy tales that I had to take out of my bedroom at night, because there was a story in it about a girl with the same name as mine—Karen—who was punished for pride in her pretty red shoes by having her feet chopped off. (And yet those shoes just kept dancing!)

It was great to discover libraries, where I could take out a book and test it to see if it was scary or good. I wanted to keep *Millions of Cats*. (The best books are the ones that get stolen most often.) But then found out I could check it out any time I wanted. And *then* I learned about the adult section!

Unless I'm about to go to another place, I seldom read travel books for information's sake. They're usually more about the traveler, i.e., *Gidget Goes Hawaiian,* and *Siddhartha,* and *The Life and Times of Kiki of Montparnasse.* Mark Twain wrote interesting and funny things about places he's been and what he did there. Now I always try to do that when I travel.

Sometimes I read about a character's experience, then forget it and don't think of it again until I'm actually having that experience or emotion. Examples: a coming-of-age story called *Christy* by Catherine Marshall, or Huxley's *The Doors of Perception.*

I know books have helped me become smarter and more creative. But I got an even better education through letters. I wrote to my older cousin and she taught me about junior high culture. I wrote to an editor who'd rejected my poems very kindly . . . and for years we wrote back and forth, teaching each other by writing back with questions and answers about our very different lives. A fringe benefit was that I'd always collect a list of books I must read, based on my pen pal's recommendation. The books we choose are almost as revealing as the letters we write. Because most of my book lists have come from men (I'm pretty popular on paper) I didn't read much by women, until I met an extraordinary librarian who turned me on to Margaret Atwood, Marge Piercy, and Lorrie Moore. She gave me whole bibliographies. That's the kind of librarian I try to be.

I come from a family of nonfiction readers. So I've read lots of magazines and reference books about hunting, engineering, birdwatching, knitting, and the encyclopedia (which my mother bought in installments, from the supermarket.) During my rebellious years, I made a point of reading the most literary things I could get my hands on. But now, more and more books take a nonfiction theme (such as salt or influenza) and throw in some really good stories—books the whole family can enjoy.

EIGHT

Fear, Love, and Everything Else

The oldest and strongest emotion
of mankind is fear.

—HOWARD PHILLIPS LOVECRAFT

Strong emotions can and do find voice in literature. Many of us experienced them via books before we ever did in "real life," and for many of us that first experience helped us deal with those same strong emotions when they did finally come our way.

Many books have helped us experience pain, ecstasy, abandonment, betrayal, and other even more frightening feelings to experience. They allow us to experience these emotions in a safe environment—because it is not, after all, real—and come to grips with them in that way. By opening our hearts to these feelings, we enrich our lives.

My mother told me once that you're never completely alone if you have a poem with you; that you can never be lonely as long as there are words you can read.

I've put her assertion to the test more frequently than I like to think. I've spent a fair amount of my life alone (and even now often seek out times when I can be alone again), but she's right: I've not been lonely. Some people turn on the TV when they need company, to keep thoughts they're not ready to confront at bay; I've always simply called to the voices that are already in my head and let the rhythm of their words seduce me. If that's not a great reason to read and memorize one's reading, I don't know what is.

> What lips these lips have kissed, and where, and why,
> I have forgotten, and what arms have lain
> Under my head till morning; but the rain
> Is full of ghosts tonight . . .
>
> —EDNA ST. VINCENT MILLAY

Memorization—just a step deeper than reading—appears these days to be a lost art. Educational pundits assure us that rote learning contributes nothing in terms of developing critical thinking. The latter assertion may be true—but there is more, surely, to education than critical thinking. There's falling in love with words. There's finding the right phrase at the right time, fitting it into a day or a moment of your life just so, like the last piece to a jigsaw puzzle, snug and right and fitting perfectly on all sides. There's hearing the echo of poets' words long after the poets are gone, but finding their expression new and vibrant and real and part of you.

That's the magic of words, surely: that they express, or at least attempt to express, all the deep swirling feelings we all experience and cannot articulate, cannot share, cannot pass along.

> Everything can change, but not the language
> that we carry inside us, like a world more exclusive
> and final than one's mother's womb.
>
> —ITALO CALVINO

Have you never been with someone, with your heart bursting, and felt the inadequacy of the words "I love you"? How many others before you have shared that feeling, and attempted to make it more, to send their words on the same gossamer wings as their feelings?

> The most powerful symptom of love is a tenderness
> which becomes at times almost insupportable.
>
> —VICTOR HUGO

Victor Hugo. My first memorization was a poem he wrote for his daughter, who had drowned—when in her teens, I believe. The poem was tragic. It never failed to bring tears to my eyes. The words were bathed in my mind in a rich luminosity, describing the innocence of a Pre-Raphaelite heroine doomed from the beginning. To be quite honest, it wasn't even Hugo's best work . . .

. . . and I couldn't get enough of it.

I muttered the verses to myself as I climbed staircases or sat in the refectory (I attended a convent school) or was supposed to be studying math. It gave me a sense of power over my environment: wherever I was, whatever I was doing, I could close my eyes and summon the words from my memory, and the rich lush images would flood my mind . . . I could fly away.

My efforts were aided by a school curriculum that included memorization as an integral part of every child's learning. Years later I remember reading of a prisoner of war in Vietnam who was grateful that he had memorized large passages of the Bible, as he felt their repetition kept him sane while staying at the Hanoi Hilton. There is something of that in the way I've looked at memorization: it's a little like carrying a library around in your head.

At school, I dutifully repeated the words as we learned them:

Racine, Molière, Chateaubriand, de la Rochfoucauld. . ... And at home I ransacked my mother's English-language books and discovered Poe and the fabulous, inimitable raven perched above the pallid bust of Pallas. I still know every word of every verse of "The Raven," and I still long for my own bust of Pallas—pallid or otherwise—to adorn my library.

She gave me Blake, too, and Elizabeth Barrett Browning and Emily Dickinson and Robert Frost. And I memorized a poem here, a thought there, until all their voices were floating around in my head, murmuring and whispering and making me try harder, write better, think more.

Not bad company to keep, on the whole.

Spirits of the Dead

There are words that you savor, that you read slowly, cherishing their feel and their meaning. And then there are words that trip over each other to get out, to keep going—tumbling off the page and into your mind.

The words of fear.

> Now are the thoughts thou shalt not banish
> Now are visions ne'er to vanish;
> From thy spirit shall they pass
> No more—like dewdrop from the grass . . .
>
> —E. A. POE

In English, Poe is the master. There can't be anything that comes close to eliciting that frisson of horror I mentioned before than reading any of his works.

I looked upon the scene before me—upon the mere house, and the simple landscape features of the domain—upon the bleak walls— upon the vacant eye-like windows—upon a few rank sedges— and upon a few white trunks of decayed trees—with an utter depression of soul which I can compare to no earthly sensation more properly than to the after-dream of the reveller upon opium— the bitter lapse into everyday life—the hideous dropping off of the veil. There was an iciness, a sinking, a sickening of the heart— an unredeemed dreariness of thought which no goading of the imagination could torture into aught of the sublime. What was it—I paused to think—what was it that so unnerved me in the contemplation of the House of Usher?

—EDGAR ALLEN POE

Poe did much more than simply instill fear in his readers; he legitimized the short story as an acceptable literary form. Moreover, he used psychology effectively in his stories, focusing on different psychological states (guilt in "The Tell-Tale Heart," fear in "The Fall of the House of Usher," for example). While he is remembered as the grand master of horror, he should also be remembered for his wide range of literary accomplishments (he wrote poetry, short stories, plays, and essays, and was in addition an editor and a critic), and indeed several cities lay claim to being "his" place.

Poe's twentieth-century successor, Howard Phillips Lovecraft, developed an original nightmarish mythology where encounters with ancient extraterrestrial intelligences bring disaster to humans who only gradually are able to see "terrifying vistas of reality, and our frightful position therein." His early stories, including "The Outsider," "The Music of Erich Zann," and "The Lurking Fear" reveal Lovecraft's ability to blur the distinction between reality and nightmare, between sanity and madness, and ultimately between what is human and what is not.

There's something in everyone that is attracted to these stories, to this frisson of fear, the cold claw raking up our spines, the sense of being watched. Psychologists say that to experience fear vicariously—by reading about it, for example, rather than actually encountering someone who wishes us harm—defuses our dread of the unknown, makes it manageable.

The appeal of the spectrally macabre is generally narrow because it demands from the reader a certain degree of imagination and a capacity for detachment from everyday life. Relatively few are free enough from the spell of the daily routine to respond to tappings from outside, and tales of ordinary feelings and events, or of common sentimental distortions of such feelings and events, will always take first place in the taste of the majority . . . But the sensitive are always with us, and sometimes a curious streak of fancy invades an obscure corner of the very hardest head; so that no amount of rationalization, reform, or Freudian analysis can quite annul the thrill of the chimney-corner whisper or the lonely wood.

—H. P. LOVECRAFT

Lovecraft and Poe, however, were writing after the "real" gothic craze had come and gone (though one does see attempts at its revival in the world of teenaged fashion, both in reading and in clothing, from time to time). The first gothic novel and the beginning of what really was an impressive literary craze, was *The Castle of Otranto*, written by Horace Walpole in 1765. It was the story of a young aristocrat who falls asleep one night and experiences feverish nightmares, revisiting the dark engravings he had been examining before he started dreaming.

Heaven nor hell shall impede my designs,
said Manfred, advancing again to seize the princess.

At that instant the portrait of his grandfather,
which hung over the bench where they had been sitting,
uttered a deep sigh and heaved its breast.

—HORACE WALPOLE

Walpole's book was succeeded by others, William Beckford's and Clara Reeve's among them, and then suddenly the genre appears to have experienced an explosion of popularity. Everyone was talking about the novels, either to defend them or to deride them. Lord Byron quipped about the people who wrote them. Jane Austen wrote an entire book (*Northanger Abbey*) dedicated to making fun of them (possibly because her own books were not faring as well as their gothic counterparts, either in advances paid by publishers or in numbers of copies sold).

But it was a woman whose work really defined the genre. *The Mysteries of Udolpho*, written by Anne Radcliffe in 1794, was an immediate bestseller . . . as were, in fact, all of her novels. A sense of evil, real evil, oozes through her work, and the reader finds his or her heartbeat quickening when a step is heard outside the room or a page needs to be turned.

Let's face it. In the 1790s, Anne Radcliffe was Stephen King.

—KYLA WARD

Women read the gothics at an alarming rate, and they wrote them at that same rate, too. Perhaps this happened because reading and writing were considered acceptable activities for a genteel lady, and thus provided an outlet for their creativity and intelligence. It's fair to say, though, that the angels and demons, the spells and horrors that flowed from these pens was anything but genteel.

Radcliffe, in any case, *was* indeed the Stephen King of her time. Her sales were outrageous; she initiated the terror/horror dichotomy discussion (again, the need to classify and therefore own bits of perception); Keats in the early eighteen-hundreds judged several of his poems to be "Radcliffian" in nature.

All of these authors, it should be noted, were writing to a formula, a technique both despised and employed today by many genre writers (sometimes, in fact, by the same genre writers!). The gothic formula, in short, consisted of the following:

- the presence of a protagonist with whom the reader can quickly and easily identify;

- action in which the protagonist is suddenly taken from her familiar surroundings and finds herself in a frightening, "other" place;

- a "castle," often literally a castle, but in reality any forbidding, isolated place;

- a succession of frightening events during which the protagonist feels herself under the spell of an unfamiliar world where the rules she has learned don't work;

- an antagonist whose motives are often unclear;

- for some reason (curiosity, desperation, need to rescue someone else, etc.), the protagonist at some point enters deeper into the horrors of the castle and learns more about its terrible secrets;

- the escape, through clever plotting or rescue.

The point of all of this is, of course, for us to fly away . . . in more ways than one. Even as we're creeping down the damp castle passage, fearful of the footfall behind us, dreading what lies ahead, we're also taking our own fears (fears about aging, about work, our children, our relationships, our bodies . . . the list can go on and on) *out* for a while. As we fear vicariously for the protagonist in the gothic novel, we learn to cope with our own fears through the simple act of experiencing them. Experiencing something takes the unknown out of the equation. We survive one set of fears, we can survive another. And grow stronger in the process.

And so the groundwork was laid for the later bearers of fear: Dracula, Frankenstein, Cthulhu . . .

. . . which leads us to Mary Shelley.

Sit back for a moment. This is a good time to brew a pot of tea or make a cup of coffee. Walk around a little; stretch. Take a deep breath, and then come back and listen while I tell you a story . . .

They have rented a lakeside villa for a wild weekend. There are five of them: a handsome playboy, his beautiful former flame, a struggling poet, a nerdy hanger-on, a mysterious literary woman. The weather isn't cooperating, but there are plenty of indoor games as compensation: an abundance of alcohol and possibly some decent drugs, very bright and talented people, and an open attitude toward both philosophy and sex.

It sounds like a rainy weekend somewhere in upstate New York in the year two thousand something, doesn't it?

But it's not. It's August of 1816. The rented space is the Villa Diodati on Lake Geneva, Switzerland. The playboy is George Gordon, Lord Byron, and the mysterious literary woman (whom he had planned to seduce) falls instead for the starving poet, Percy Bysshe Shelley. The group is playing the kind of games one plays when people have been awake together for twenty hours; they eventually end up gambling, a wager inspired by the thunder and lightning and their own bravado.

Who, they challenge each other, can tell the best ghost story?

Byron makes an erratic attempt at a story later reshaped for publication by his nerdy friend, the physician John Polidori, a story that will ultimately be told in its finest form forty years later by Bram Stoker.

Polidori himself recounts the tale: "Began my ghost story after tea. Twelve o'clock, really began to talk ghostly. L. B. repeated some verses of Coleridge's 'Christabel,' of the witch's breast; when silence ensued, and Shelley, suddenly shrieking and putting his hands to his head, ran out of the room with a candle. Threw water in his face, and after gave him ether. He was looking at Mrs. S., and suddenly thought of a woman he had heard of who had eyes instead of nipples, which, taking hold of his mind, horrified him."

And as the party continues, the bluestocking shuts herself off in a tower room and wonders what would happen if the ghost they all fear were not external. What would happen if the horror were something inside? . . .

She will marry the poet and take his name just before the book she began on that night is published. Her name is Mary Wollstonecraft Shelley, and her "little ghost story" is *Frankenstein*.

Shelley opened up a new look at the genre that would obsess writers from her time to ours: the concept of the darkness within, the knowledge that much of what we have to fear lies, not somewhere "out there," but in fact within ourselves. Knowledge is both the source of light and the source of darkness. "What could not be expected in the country of eternal light?" asks Walton, seizing upon science as the ultimate good. The novel, though, goes on to raise the question: Just because we can do something, should we?

What Shelley opened up was the greatest fear of all—the fear of what is within.

I've said it before and I'll say it again in this context, to the consternation of many readers, no doubt: we read to lose ourselves, and we read to find ourselves. *We* are the doctor who created the monster out of what was within himself; we are the monster, too. Whether it is our imagination or the society around us that forms the cauldron or laboratory test tubes, the result is the same: until we can face our own darkness, that which is inside of us that we keep denying, keep repressing, keep ignoring, then we'll never be whole. Transparency is freedom.

Frankenstein's subtitle is "The Modern Prometheus," and playing with fire is more than an expression in Shelley's world, as it perhaps should be in ours. That which brings light can also burn, and its loss plunges us into darkness. These are places where few dare to tread: the scientist, the priest . . . and the novelist.

Creating the Monster

Let's Talk About Love

It's not such a difficult segue from the literature of fear to the literature of love: the way was paved by none other than Lord Byron and Percy Shelley themselves.

Byron was a shameless self-marketer, living a dissolute life and determined to be seen as such, but he also produced some of the most beautiful words that touch any heart that has ever known love.

> She walks in beauty, like the night
> Of cloudless climes and starry skies;
> And all that's best of dark and bright
> Meet in her aspect and her eyes . . .

Byron was the rock star of the first years of the nineteenth century, and like any rock star, he consciously lived up to his image. Gossips found new material to discuss every day. Word had it—my dear, can you *believe* it?—that he'd murdered one of his mistresses and then used her skull as a cup to drink her blood! Oh, you don't say . . .

And perhaps it *was* a little over the top to name his perfectly legitimate daughter Ada after a former girlfriend—oops. (The daughter went on to become Countess Lovelace and the first computer programmer, working with Charles Babbage on the Difference Engine; it's amazing how often the lives of interesting people intersect.)

And I'm not entirely sure what exactly to make of his letters from Venice in which he claims to have spent twenty-five hundred pounds in two years on sex "of one kind or another." Well, just remember that *Childe Harold's Pilgrimage* was largely autobiographical, and that should say it all.

But Byron also traveled through Greece to Constantinople and the Turkish courts, rode through the wilds of Albania and climbed the Swiss Alps, no mean feats at his time.

And, perhaps most importantly, Byron probably didn't need to live a dissolute life in such a determinedly public way: his words continue to enchant and seduce, to endure in ways that would probably amaze—and delight—the poet himself, could he but see it happening.

Today he's put in a niche along with the rest of the so-called "romantic poets"—William Blake, Samuel Taylor Coleridge, Percy Bysshe Shelley, William Wordsworth, John Keats, Alphonse de Lamartine, Victor Hugo, Théophile Gautier, Charles Baudelaire, Ralph Waldo Emerson, Henry Wadsworth Longfellow, Robert Burns, Walt Whitman—though we do them all a disservice to limit the term "romantic" to our own latter-day narrow definition of the word.

Romantic poetry is not about romance per se, but rather about a return to nature (which is most obvious in Wordsworth's work). Romantic poets were reacting against the industrial revolution and the enlightenment, which they felt placed too much emphasis on reason over emotion. So the romance is less about flowers and sonnets for the beloved than it is . . . well, about flowers and sonnets in general.

Still, we need to wend our way back to love.

Most people in the English-speaking world are introduced to writings about love through Shakespeare, and there truly is nothing that can compete with his star-crossed lovers.

On the other hand, he did set up a situation that has provided a blueprint for love stories for centuries to come. The reality is that a happy love story—while something we may all wish to *live*—can (and does) quickly become stiflingly boring when it's in a book. Literature thrives on conflict. And conflicted lovers are a perennial favorite.

Love never dies a natural death. It dies because we
don't know how to replenish its source. It dies of blindness
and errors and betrayals. It dies of illness and wounds;
it dies of weariness, of withering, of tarnishing.

—ANAÏS NIN

Spiritual Passion

Our spirituality is as much a part of us as are our sexual and
romantic passions, as are our fears. All of this is really just another
way of talking about transcendence. We transcend the ordinariness
and banality of our daily lives through our passions: through our
fears and our loves and our sense of Something Other, something
beyond.

We define our spirituality according to our beliefs and experiences, and some of us deny them altogether. It seems clear,
however, that all people have a need of—and a passion about—
something that is bigger than ourselves. In a letter to his brother,
the artist Vincent van Gogh wrote, "That does not keep me from
having a terrible need of—shall I say the word?—religion. Then I
go out at night to paint the stars."

The atheist too has his moments of shuddering misgiving, of an all
but irresistible suspicion that the old tales may after all be true,
that something or someone from outside may at any moment
break into his neat, explicable, mechanical universe.

—C. S. LEWIS

I am only deeply familiar with my own spiritual tradition, but
perhaps as you read this you can draw some parallels with whatever belief system you espouse, whatever spiritual tradition is
yours. And at the end of the day, many, many religions have the

same principles, though they may be articulated differently. How far, indeed, is the Wiccan *What you do comes back to you times three*, from the Buddhist notion of karma or the Christian ideal of treating others as you'd like to be treated?

Passion will always find its way into words, and poetry is perhaps the best vehicle for expressing passion. Read T. S. Eliot, for example. "Ash Wednesday" is filled with spiritual passion. "Will the veiled sister pray . . . for children at the gate, who will not go away and cannot pray . . . pray for those who chose and oppose."

> The chill ascends from feet to knees,
> The fever sings in mental wires.
> If to be warmed, then I must freeze
> And quake in frigid purgatorial fires
> Of which the flame is roses, and the smoke is briars.
>
> —T. S. ELIOT

The writings of Julian of Norwich, a mystic and an anchoress (an anchorite/anchoress is a sort of hermit who lives in a cell connected to a public church, sometimes available for religious counsel while still maintaining a solitary life) who lived in the late fourteenth and early fifteenth century, are filled with an ecstatic love grounded in reality; she wrote that suffering is not a punishment, but rather a means of becoming closer to God—a radical departure from the accepted theology of her time.

Another mystic, the Carmelite St. John of the Cross, wrote very passionately indeed of a dark night of the soul, the despair through which we sometimes pass in order to attain enlightenment, closeness to God, spiritual ecstasy.

Mysticism is the passionate side of religion. In my previous Open Your Heart book I quoted Frederick Buechner in *Wishful Thinking*, who said in part, "Religions start, as Frost said poems do, with a lump in the throat." Mysticism is the feeling side of things, unrelated to dogma or theology, the absolute delight or absolute terror that are the extremes of love. So to read about the passion of spirituality, you could do worse than to read about mysticism.

While the word passion is foreign in many ways to Buddhism, the goal of enlightenment is consonant, to my mind at least, with the sense of awakening experienced by mystics.

The groups of Taoist texts include journeys to places where reason cannot go: the cavern of the realized, the cavern of the mysterious, the cavern of the spirit.

We cannot speak of mysticism without looking briefly at some other mystical spirituality: at the Kabbalah, the "gathering of sparks" that comes out of Jewish tradition, and Sufism, which broke with Islam in proclaiming the importance of mystical experiences and the inability of language to access those experiences. There are a number of writings available in both areas (search engines are your friend) that I invite you to explore.

My own tradition—Catholicism—is rich with verbal imagery on the subject of love and religious ecstasy. The image of Christ as bridegroom and Church as bride has long been part of the Church's self-identity, and many of our saints and mystics have indeed very clearly been in love with God.

But the reality is that magic happens everywhere. Anyone who has any spiritual tradition has felt it—that lump in the throat, that tug of another world, that moment of blinding clarity—and even when our workaday selves ignore those experiences, or deny them, we know in the secret places inside ourselves that they are, perhaps, the most real of our reality, the truest expression of our inner selves.

Perhaps the best translators, so to speak, of mysticism are the poets; poetry, with its rich imagery and its ability to hint at truth without defining it, is a natural vehicle for mystical knowledge and understanding.

Jalalud'din Rumi wrote a wide range of inspiring and devotional poetry expressing the Sufi's experience of union with the divine; Rumi has become one of the world's most popular poets. His funeral (lasting forty days!) was attended by Muslims, Jews, Persians, Christians, and Greeks.

> We are as the flute, and the music in us is from thee;
> we are as the mountain and the echo in us is from thee.
>
> —RUMI

St. Teresa of Ávila had trouble sitting through her devotions and remarked once that the end of the hour's prayer couldn't come soon enough. Eventually, however, she was so filled with divine contemplation that at times her body would spontaneously levitate. Teresa felt these miracles to be slightly ostentatious and when she felt the levitation happening, she asked her sisters to sit on her. Enough was apparently enough.

I've always liked Teresa. One of her sayings indicates how spirituality and everyday life are so intimately intertwined: "No wonder you have so few friends," she complained one day to God. "Look at how you treat the ones you do have!"

> Let nothing upset you,
> let nothing startle you.
> All things pass;
> God does not change.
> Patience wins all it seeks.
> Whoever has God
> lacks nothing:
> God alone is enough.
>
> —ST. TERESA OF ÁVILA

Thomas Merton wrote over sixty other books and hundreds of poems and articles on topics ranging from monastic spirituality to civil rights, nonviolence, and the nuclear arms race. During his last years, he became deeply interested in Asian religions, particularly Buddhism, and in promoting East-West dialogue.

> Wind and a bobwhite
> And the afternoon sun.
> By ceasing to question the sun
> I have become light,
> Bird and wind.
> My leaves sing.
>
> —THOMAS MERTON

Sri Ramakrishna represents the spirituality of the seers and sages of India, living in uninterrupted contemplation of God. He reached a depth of God-consciousness that transcends all time and place and has a universal appeal. Those who seek God—from all religions—feel irresistibly drawn to his life and teachings.

> You see many stars in the sky at night,
> but not when the sun rises. Can you therefore say
> that there are no stars in the heavens during the day?
> Friends, similarly you cannot see God because of your
> ignorance, but say not that there is no God.
>
> —SRI RAMAKRISHNA

Zen masters teach that the pure mind is the eternal Buddha-nature. To attain enlightenment, to be aware of one's own Buddha-nature, it is necessary to go beyond our ordinary thoughts. Zen masters often appear to be talking in riddles as they tried to point toward one's Buddha nature—a consciousness at once pervasive and elusive.

Confused by thoughts,
we experience duality in life.
Unencumbered by ideas,
the enlightened see the one Reality.

—HUI-NENG

Han Shan was a hermit and poet of the Tang Dynasty who fled the aftermath of the An Lu-shan rebellion in 760 and retreated to the mountains of eastern China. In his later years, people thought of Han Shan in a variety of ways—as an eccentric Taoist, crazy saint, ascetic mystic, and wise fool.

People ask for the road to Cold Mountain,
but no road reaches Cold Mountain.
Summer sky-still ice won't melt.
The sun comes out but gets obscured by mist.
Imitating me, where does that get you?
My mind isn't like yours.
When your mind is like mine
you can enter here.

—HAN SHAN

The political events of the 11th century—an unstable military empire, unease as an orthodox Muslim state was evolving—played a major role in the course of Omar Khayyam's life. Outside the world of mathematics, Khayyam is best known as a result of Edward Fitzgerald's popular translation of nearly 600 short four-line poems composing the *Rubaiyat*.

The Moving Finger writes, and, having writ,
Moves on: nor all thy Piety nor Wit
Shall lure it back to cancel half a Line,
Nor all thy Tears wash out a Word of it.

—OMAR KHAYYAM

READING EXERCISE

What gets you excited? What makes you passionate? What's the strongest emotion you've experienced recently?

Take a moment and write it down. Remember the feeling—delight or anger, joy or pain, whatever it is. Sit with the feeling for a while. How would you express it?

Now go to a library or the Internet and find a book, a poem, a short story that deals with that same emotion.

Read it. Did it bring you closer to your own feelings?

There are as many ways to express strong emotion as there are emotions. Explore what words bring you closest to your own true feelings.

NINE

Imagination: Coming Full Circle

> Reading supplies bread for imagination to feed on,
> and bones for it to chew on.
>
> —ALEX OSBORN

We all know that we enjoy reading. But does reading really *do* anything for us? Does it make us better people? Smarter people? More creative people? Let's come to grips with what the experts are saying about reading and the imagination.

Michael LeBoeuf, in his wonderful book *Creative Thinking*, asserts that any primary ability or talent can be developed by training, and that people can improve their creative ability by exercising it. And you can start exercising it by reading—but only by reading selectively and actively.

How can reading help the imagination? It does so when you get involved—with the story, with the subject, with wondering what the connections between what you're reading and your "real life" are. Example? Read a biography (not a memoir; memoirs are subjective and pull you into the writer's frame of reference. For this exercise, you need the objectivity of a third person's point of view.); any life worth documenting usually involves something significant; how can that something be translated into your life, your times?

Or find something that interests you. Politics, philosophy, history. Read everything that you can find about your subject of interest. Do you remember John Smith, the author of the *Wapiti-Hoo*, who we met in chapter one? Remember how he devoted a year of his life completely to the study of one subject? That may be more intense concentration than you're willing to give, but at least find and read several points of view on the matter and consider them all before making up your own mind about the topic.

I did this once when I first read Josephine Tey's *The Daughter of Time,* an historical exploration masquerading as a mystery novel. Tey had me completely convinced by the end of it that Richard III had been sorely maligned, first by the historians of his time, and then later (taking his cue from said historians) by Shakespeare, the latter truly screwing down the lid of the coffin of public opinion.

I was outraged.

The princes in the tower? Killed by their uncle Richard? Nonsense, claimed Tey: he had no reason to have them murdered . . . but the Tudors did. The first accusation of the terrible murder is made by Sir Thomas More, writing long after the events—and at the Tudor royal court.

Ah, politics.

I launched myself into a personal quest: a rehabilitate-Richard campaign. But not before trying to learn what the other side had to say—I think it's known as "discovery," were we opposing attorneys preparing our cases. So I read Alison Weir's well-written (but ultimately, I thought, unconvincing) *The Princes in the Tower,* arguing for the traditionalist point of view.

The traditionalist point of view got its best shot of public relations in 1592:

And therefore, since I cannot prove a lover
To entertain these fair well-spoken days,
I am determined to prove a villain
And hate the idle pleasures of these days.
Plans have I laid, inductions dangerous,
By drunken prophecies, libels, and dreams,
To set my brother Clarence and the King
In deadly hate the one against the other.

—WILLIAM SHAKESPEARE

So: the jury is out about Richard, I suppose, but it was a good exercise for me, reading Sir Thomas More's disputed biography, Shakespeare's extraordinary if partisan play, more modern scholars. An interesting and—yes, creative—mental exercise.

Yours, now, to try. Find something controversial in history or science or politics (and if you cannot find anything in any of those three fields that is of interest to you, you're not looking hard enough), and make it a point to find out everything that you can about it. Take a page from the debate clubs and prepare a brilliant and logical argument supporting one side, and then the other.

Don't look now, but you just exercised your creative side, fed your knowledge-hungry side, and in the process . . . you flew away.

"Last night there were four Marys . . ."

Nancy Pearl reports that Anna Quindlen once said, in response to a question about her favorite authors, that she read "the Alices." Quindlen didn't specify which ones to which she was referring, but a quick list might include Alice Hoffman, Alice Munro, Alice Walker, Alice Sebold, Alice Adams, Alice Mattison . . . and probably many more that I'm forgetting.

Is there something to that? Would you agree? Who would you add to the list?

What are the first names of your favorite authors? Are they all, like Quindlen's list, Anglo-Saxon names? Are any of them? What do their names tell you about your reading comfort zone?

Can you challenge yourself to step out of it?

Try that: make a list of your favorite authors' names. Not the book titles, not the genres, not anything else: just the names. See if you can discern a pattern. Are most of them male? Female? Are there Russian names, French names, Latino names? There's no right answer here; it's just an exercise.

If there is a pattern, there's nothing wrong with it: what you like is entirely your own affair. But I've always been an advocate of shaking things up a bit, so try this next. If there's something missing from your list—if it didn't include any Latin American authors, for example—make it a point to read something written by one of the "missing" authors. Not an entire opus, and not a lot of books: just one thing. A short story. A biography. Something. Anything.

At the end of the day, this new author still might not make it onto your list of favorite authors. Or he or she might. It really doesn't matter: what matters is that you were able to step outside of your comfort zone, try something different, stretch your mind, challenge your thinking.

I've been doing this lately with music. Since the advent of the iTunes Music Store and the possibility of obtaining one song from an unfamiliar artist (as opposed to the expense of buying an entire album), I've been stretching my listening boundaries. I travel a great deal, so for each trip I download two new songs from artists I've not listened to before. Not enough to be overwhelmed, just enough to sample and see how I feel about them.

There are some I've not listened to since that first trial period. There have been others I've come to appreciate and even love, though, and all because of a deliberate decision to step outside of my comfort zone.

It's not a bad way to meet new authors. Try short stories or essays to start with (less commitment than there is in a whole novel or book!) and see if there are one or two who catch your attention, seduce you, lead you on, make you want more.

There's never a bad time to step out of your rut.

Words, Words, Words

Reading doesn't need to mean books. Magazines can be wonderful springboards for creativity. Oddly enough, one possible source of ideas is the *Reader's Digest,* praised by none other than the creative genius himself, Walt Disney: "Your imagination may be creaky or timid or dwarfed or frozen at points," he said. "The *Reader's Digest* can serve as a gymnasium for its training."

It may not be considered classic, but there is something to Disney's perception. Pick up any issue of the magazine and you'll see a plethora of ideas: quotations, quizzes, short humorous pieces, vocabulary development, and stories about places, people, real-life drama, and science. There's something there for everyone, explaining perhaps why it's a perennial favorite for medical waiting rooms.

The reading room of the public library is a terrific place to explore magazines. Don't go there and read the magazines you're accustomed to read: challenge yourself! Pick up a magazine for Muslim women (as I did recently), or something about gardening, or cars, or anime . . . anything that's outside of your usual experience and interests. Look for literary magazines such as *Zoetrope: All-Story, The Paris Review, Ploughshares,* or *Glimmer Train,* and read a short story or two. Pick up an arts magazine and see if any of the pictures inspire you. Read the latest gossip, even if you've never heard of the people involved.

The point is, use magazines to jump-start your own creativity, to read something that will be a little outside of the ordinary, something that will help you think differently about the world around you.

Because that's the greatest creativity there is.

> I have sometimes dreamt . . . that when the Day of Judgment dawns and the great conquerors and lawyers and statesmen come to receive their rewards—their crowns, their laurels, their names carved indelibly upon imperishable marble— the Almighty will turn to Peter and will say, not without a certain envy when He sees us coming with our books under our arms, "Look, these need no reward. We have nothing to give them here. They have loved reading."
>
> —VIRGINIA WOOLF

I told a friend that I was writing this chapter, and she laughed. "Creativity doesn't have anything to do with reading," she said. "Reading is reacting. It's writing that's creative."

You have to really stop and think when you hear something like that. Is it a result of the couch-potato phenomenon, this assumption that being receptive is passive, lethargic, unengaged? *Au contraire:* to read is to become part of something else, something bigger than yourself and your life. "We read," says Harold Bloom, "frequently if unknowingly in quest of a mind more original than our own." And it's Jean-Paul Sartre who once said that to read a book is to write it.

All of life is, ultimately, a journey of self-discovery. We are the most fascinating creatures of our own universe, and we try to mold our lives, our thoughts, our surroundings around the self we want to become, the self we want others to perceive in us. So it's natural that this fascination with self expresses itself through the words we choose to read.

> These come to me days and nights and go from me again,
> But they are not the Me myself.
>
> Apart from the pulling and hauling stands what I am,
> Stands amused, complacent, compassionating, idle, unitary,
> Looks down, is erect, or bends an arm on an impalpable certain rest,
> Looking with side-curved head curious what will come next,
> Both in and out of the game and watching and wondering at it.
>
> —WALT WHITMAN

We read, and we watch ourselves read, and we look to find ourselves in the words that we read—and all the while, our creative minds and hearts are at work, redefining ourselves as we take in new perceptions, new information, even new words.

We are never the same person after reading a book that we were before.

Style

We cannot discuss imagination, I think, without discussing style.

In English, we tend to make a distinction between literary language and spoken language, but the style of writing we find in books stretches along a continuum between formal and informal, depending on the content and the intended audience. A literary novel may be written in a formal style, while the dialogue used by the characters populating the novel could be more informal, colloquial—even incorrect; dialogue, if well written, reflects the language of the characters using it, and it helps the reader understand those characters.

A book written for a scholarly audience will have a different style and tone than one that gives dating tips. (I should know: I've edited both, and my favorite was the latter, two hundred-odd pages that boiled down to two succinct pieces of advice: know your date's name, and make sure your fingernails are clean. Not bad guidance at that!)

But style goes beyond grammar and correct—or incorrect—usage: style is one of the reasons we stay up late at night reading, why we pick up one book over another at the library, why we like one author but are indifferent to another. Along with Supreme Justice Potter, we may not be able to define the style we like, but we know it when we see it.

In an age when other fantastically speedy, widespread media are triumphing and running the risk of flattening all communication onto a single, homogeneous surface, the function of literature is communication between things that are different simply because they are different, not blunting but even sharpening the differences between them, following the true bent of the written language.

—ITALO CALVINO

Style is of particular importance, surprisingly enough, in genre fiction. An amazingly prescient book by Neal Stephenson, *Snow Crash,* is one that Paul likes quite a lot and rereads at regular intervals. And I've attempted to read it at regular intervals as well. Stephenson is a master at what he does and has captured a particular specific voice so important to telling a story well . . . and it's just not a voice that I feel comfortable reading. It's difficult. It's challenging. And someday I will read it, but in the meantime there are many readers who seek out that voice, who thrive on it, who find it communicating directly with them.

Which is one of the reasons we all head to different areas of the bookshop or library, I suppose!

Creative Reading

Those who study such things will admit that they don't know a lot about the creative process that takes place when a person is reading—especially reading fiction. Library scholar Louise Glenn, however, has suggested that readers in fact create their own reading experience. "Findings," she reports, "indicated that readers played an important creative role in the reading experience, with the majority of readers identifying the existence of a creative partnership between the reader and the writer."

Actually, up until the twentieth century, most thoughtful people believed that reading fiction could have harmful repercussions in the reader's life. Cultural institutions felt threatened by some of the views of society articulated in fiction, while some psychologists feared that people would spend their time enjoying life vicariously instead of through active participation in it.

As the twentieth century advanced, literary fiction was given a pass, but popular fiction continued to receive the same negative perception, and the effect—as you can well imagine—was the marginalization of readers. Literary (or "good") fiction became the province of critics, theorists, and academics, while popular (or "bad") fiction belonged to people who weren't clever or highbrow enough to read the "real" literary works.

One imagines two sets of bookcases in people's homes: the one in the living room filled with classic works, and the one in the bedroom with popular (and thus in many minds, "trashy") fiction on its shelves.

Or did I just describe your house? The reality is that we still tend to make these distinctions in our minds, judging ourselves and others through an empirically flawed and totally unnecessary set of artificial standards. We take the so-called superiority of literary fiction for granted and behave as though our volumes of genre fiction, for example, are slightly embarrassing. "It's what I read when I'm tired," we say when we finally do get around to admitting to an enjoyment of science fiction or romance or mysteries. "I know it's not serious, but it's fun."

The implication being, in case you didn't catch it, that literary fiction is indeed serious—and is not very much fun at all.

Enter Rachel Van Riel and Chris Meade, who contend strongly that the reader doesn't just absorb the writer's original thoughts passively, but rather takes an active role in the reading process. Van Riel is the founder of Opening the Book, a reader development organization, and together with Meade has developed what they call a "new aesthetic of reading." Setting up the physical space in which people read (for example, in schools and libraries) with this creative process in mind can help people read better, read more creatively, and assimilate what they have read.

The reality is that reading has not been traditionally perceived as a creative activity. In fact, participants in one study saw it as quite the opposite: "I wonder if I would create things if I wasn't spending so much time reading . . . you know, whether we'd all be making our own clothes and decorating our own houses . . . You read in the time you should have put aside for doing something really creative." Others pointed to reading as not being creative because there is not physical output.

Amazing: reading as an impediment to creativity!

Yet these same respondents all saw that creation of and immersion in a narrative world is the greatest gift of fiction—that ability of the novel or story to transport readers into another world. And once you understand that engagement as the beginning of a creative process, the rest falls into place: because once the reader enters into the story, the story in some ways becomes the reader's. The reader starts imagining the characters, no doubt differently than the author imagined them; the reader sees places, interactions, relationships that the author may not have seen or been aware of; it's the reader who, in a real way, interacts with the text in real time. The author writes and moves on; the reader sifts and thinks and reacts and imagines.

> Imaginative readers rewrite books to suit their own taste,
> omitting and mentally altering as they read.
>
> —GRAVES & HODGE

The reader brings all of his or her experiences, knowledge, beliefs and prejudices to his or her reading, so that no two people will react in precisely the same way to any book, and no two readings will be exactly the same. We've all encountered the situation in which we've returned to a beloved book after a period of years to find—with such disappointment!—that it no longer thrills or excites us the way it did. We are not the same; we are, in essence, two separate readers, and so we bring a different viewpoint to the reading experience.

It's one of the reasons that book groups can be so rewarding. Because we each see different things in a story, and in fact pull more things *out* of the story, our reading can be enriched to an extraordinary extent by hearing and taking in the reading experiences of others.

Whether assimilating a story alone or as part of a reading group or book club, you will find that the creative process, if it's really been activated, doesn't stop when you shut the book or read the last page. The story, the characters, the situations, the dilemmas presented—they all stay with you and chances are very good that they will have some impact on your own life, your thinking, your way of looking at things.

They all stay with you.

Think of all you would never have experienced if you had not
learned to read—readers are at home in the life of the mind;
they live with ideas as well as events and facts . . .
Literate adults make their reading work for them.

—JUDITH ELKIN

Once you meet a character in a book, once you explore a landscape in a book, it becomes part of you forever. The character becomes someone that you know, the landscape—what Eleanor Cameron has called "the country of the mind"—becomes something familiar to you, a part of your inner history, your inner being.

Some people can access that inner life through meditation or contemplation; many others enter it through reading.

Have you ever noticed, when you pick up a book to reread that you'd once read many years ago, how suddenly that other time comes flooding back? The smells, the sounds, the feelings engulf you. That time has remained stored in that book, in those words, and all you needed to access it again was to reread them.

> There are perhaps no days of our childhood we lived so fully
> as those we believe we left without having lived them,
> those we spent with a favorite book.
>
> —MARCEL PROUST

Don't look now, but all of what I just talked about is part of the creative process. It's you interacting with a book at so many different levels that it's sometimes hard to pry them apart. There's a relationship that develops between the reader and the story that is unique to that person at that time in his or her life. You bring all of who you are—all your experiences, all your thoughts, all your being—to the interaction between you and the story, and since you are constantly changing, growing, incorporating new information and experiences into your repertoire, you can pick up the same story at a different time and get something different out of it, simply because you're bringing something different to it.

In a way, the reader is more active and more creative than the writer in this regard. The writer interacted with the story in the time it took him or her to think about it, mull it over, write and rewrite it. But once the story is finished (we generally call this "publication"), the writer stopped the interaction. The reader, on the other hand, can go back over and over again to continue to interact with the story and may, therefore, have a deeper and more ongoing relationship with it.

When you read some books, they seem to be aimed directly at you—have you noticed that? Did the author know that someone like you was out there, or did he or she capture something universal, a bit of wisdom that works for everyone?

Or does the book or story capture you because of what you, the reader, have brought to it?

I'm not sure that there are any definitive answers to any of these questions. I think that the truth—if there is such a thing—lies, as usual, in the cracks, the in-between places that we don't define and generally don't even think about. The questions may not even have any answers.

But I do think that they're worth thinking about as you explore your own creativity and how you bring it to bear on what you read.

Finally, when you stop and think about it, books really are about the reader; the act of writing expects something of the act of reading. An author writes for the response that will be elicited from the reader—an emotion, an action, even a reaction of some sort. From start to finish, a book's focus is on the reader . . . is on you. It's up to you to be creative enough to respond.

READING EXERCISE

There is substantial research exploring the interaction between reader and text, but we still actually know very little about the process or how it can inform our own intellectual lives.

So it's time to do our own research!

Choose a book—novel, memoir, something nonfiction about a topic that's of interest to you. Before you open it, sit with it for a moment. Think about who you are right now, where you are. For example, you might be thinking, "I'm thirty-four years old, and that's important to me because I just had a birthday. I have a terrific family but I don't always have the time I'd like to spend with them. I'm hoping for a promotion at work. I have a stack of books I want to read that I haven't gotten to."

Then go just a little deeper. Who are you right at this moment? "I'm feeling a little hurt because my brother didn't send me a birthday card this year. It makes me think about my relationship with him, where we've been together, what it's been like lately. Maybe that means I'm not as sure of myself as I'd like people to think, 'cause if my own brother forgets my birthday, I have to wonder what's going on."

You get my drift. Think about yourself, who you are in this particular moment. What is it that you're looking forward to? Is there anything you're feeling unsettled about? What was the last perfectly wonderful thing that happened to you? *Who are you*?

And now open the book and start to read.

Read enough to get involved, to really immerse yourself in the story or subject matter. A chapter, maybe two. Then stop. Mark your place, and close the book. (I mean that: really close the book—there's a connection between our physical acts and how we process and think about things.)

Think about the issues you had in your mind before you opened the book, and revisit them now. Does anything seem different? Can you think of a new angle, another way of looking at the problem?

Maybe there's nothing, and you need to read on. But it's my experience that if you really put your problems, issues, thoughts, sense of self in the forefront of your mind before you begin to read, then something will happen. It could be as simple as part of your brain sorting things while the rest of it is occupied reading. Or it could mean that the effort of creatively interacting with the text draws creativity to the other, problem-solving part of you.

Either way, I think you'll find it works.

Thoughts about Reading . . . with Sharon Darling

Teacher, administrator, and educational entrepreneur are all titles Sharon Darling wears as she challenges the status quo and develops new methods of educating families.

Darling is president and founder of the National Center for Family Literacy (NCFL). Located in Louisville, Kentucky, NCFL is internationally recognized as the leader in the field of family literacy, and is well known for placing family literacy—parents and children learning together—on the agenda for social change.

What made you get involved in literacy work?

As a second-grade teacher, I witnessed firsthand the difference between kids whose parents where involved in their education and those whose parents were not. And it was evident that a child's success was greatly influenced by their first and best teachers, the parents.

Since then, countless research studies have shown that even when societal factors such as poverty and unemployment are in the equation, parents who partner with teachers to foster a child's educational development pave the road for opportunity. Children from these environments can compete in the classroom with students from the "other side of the tracks."

My personal goal was to foster and develop a learning model where parents and children worked together in the child's school and capitalized on learning activities in the home. That model continues to influence national education policy and legislation. More importantly, the model has fueled NCFL's ability to positively impact the lives of over 1 million families since our inception in 1989.

What do books and reading mean to you personally?

The ability to read is literally the gateway to all life has to offer.

Because reading is the foundation of successful educational progress, it is important that we not only provide books, but tips based on scientifically based reading research that parents and educators can instill in young readers to keep them interested in broadening their horizons.

Do you remember your first book?

Yes, but I can't recall the name. I remember it because it was about a little girl walking through the leaves in fall and the wonderful noises they made and the description of the smells of autumn. I probably remember it most because my mother read it to me as I sat in her soft lap.

What is the value of storytelling in a culture?

Storytelling is important for a number of reasons.

Sharing stories with our children has always been a source of inspiration, for them and for us as adults. Through talking and reading, we help children learn about and understand the world around them, and to think about the choices they make. At the same time, the questions children ask can bring a whole new perspective to our lives as adults.

On the surface and in the short term, a child sitting at the feet of parents or grandparents is gaining understanding of his family . . . where they came from, what it was like for them growing up, what they have accomplished.

Quality of life begins at home. It is no coincidence that education begins at home, too.

What are the obstacles to literacy? How can people help?

As a nation, we should be concerned that more than 34 million adults in this country lack the literacy skills to complete a job application, vote, or read a bedtime story to a child.

Poverty and low literacy are indisputably connected. Many parents who find it hard to support their families financially also face enormous challenges when trying to support their children's language and literacy development.

Poverty creates its own priorities, and parents who are facing the many challenges of poverty often don't view education as a priority—either for themselves or for their children.

There are many ways to help others reach their goals—by volunteering in an adult literacy program, tutoring children in an after-school program, or advocating for families in your community.

One of the greatest ways adults inspire new generations is by example. Making literacy a priority for your family will inspire thoughtful, well-informed, engaged generations to come.

What book or author has influenced you the most? In what way?

There Are No Children Here, written by Alex Kotlowitz. I read the book at a time when the sacrifices I had made to further family literacy were beginning to take a toll on me personally. The efforts seemed to be miniscule in relation to the challenges of illiteracy, inequity, and poverty. *There Are No Children Here* renewed my commitment and reinvigorated my passion.

What is the role/value of reading in a person's life?

Adults with good literacy skills can read the want ads in the newspaper, fill out job applications, find directions on a map. They can do everything they need to provide for their families and themselves. They can also greatly enrich the quality of their lives.

TEN

Nonfiction Themes

['ve tried to steer away from dividing this book into fiction and nonfiction categories; if you've been reading with your eyes and heart open you'll have realized by now that I dislike categories altogether and especially try not to classify anything via the white/ black, yes/no, fiction/nonfiction way of thinking. Binary thinking doesn't fit particularly well in a nonbinary world.

But there are many books that simply don't fit into any of the ways I've organized the material up until now, and so for them: ta-da! Their own chapter!

Moreover, there's some subject matter that's best dealt with in nonfiction—or would take an exceptional novelist to pull off in a fictional context. One such subject is stories of horrendous child-hoods—*A Child Called "It"* is probably the easiest example, but also Ishmael Beah's *A Long Way Gone*, or even Harry Crews's *A Child-hood* (which wasn't as terrible as the others, but should be read any-way for the sheer gorgeousness of the language.). It may be difficult to write effectively about such things in novel-length fiction with-out running the risk of being exploitative.

And then there's the whole arena of scholarly books, which isn't really the focus of *this* book, but bears some thought. As someone with a number of graduate degrees, I'm obviously grateful for the well-researched, well-written and, frankly, exciting books I've studied. Don't discount them in terms of opening your heart, either. You'll find wisdom in the most unexpected places.

Self-help Books

In general, I hate them. This probably sounds odd coming from someone whose books in this series could conceivably be categorized as self-help, but it seems to me that a whole lot of self-help books are meant to:

- make you feel good, leaning heavily on pseudo case studies;
- tell you something incredibly obvious, leaning heavily on pseudo case studies;
- make the author a lot of money;
- all of the above.

Which is not to say that there isn't a time and a place for them. Indeed, I've given out more copies of the slim volume *How to Survive the Loss of a Love* than I can remember. I found it helpful, at one time, and think it can be useful to others going through a death (whether of an individual or of a relationship).

But in general they often seem to have the same content, just packaged differently. Or so I tended to think until I read Richard Carlson and Joseph Bailey's *Slowing Down to the Speed of Life*. And found that it seemed to speak, very directly, to . . . me.

Which of course got me to reexamine my previous attitude. I suspect that there are other books out there—probably more than a few of them—that say approximately the same thing: slow down, live in the moment, be conscious of what is around you, know that you can change your thoughts. I'd probably read it dozens of times before in various incarnations of its message. This one caught me, was written in language I was ready to hear.

Was it the same thing, packaged differently? Of course it was. And the packaging *does* count, does make a difference. Different authors are able to reach different people in different ways.

So I'm not quite as condescending about self-help books as I used to be. (Actually, I'm not as condescending about a lot of things as I used to be; maybe I'm finally growing up!) And there's a huge lesson in that, I think. There's a reason there are so many millions of books out there, more than there have ever been, with still more pouring off the presses every day.

Maybe it's because in an increasingly technological age we're moving away from the centers of wisdom that used to be provided by extended family, by a rich network of friends, by our own life experiences. What in many of these books appears to be common sense may not be accessible as such to a lot of people; yet they're able to access the knowledge through reading.

Certainly one of the greatest strengths of self-help books is to assure people that they're not alone. In an earlier chapter I spoke of finding myself in the words of an Anita Shreve novel, but you can find yourself, too, in self-help books. Perhaps you didn't realize that there are other people out there who grew up with an alcoholic parent, or who struggle with shyness, or who get into self-destructive relationships. In the self-help section of the bookshop, you'll find people like you who have shared these experiences—and found ways of surviving, means of coping. And we can all learn a lot from someone who has already been there.

And that leads us naturally into talking about memoirs . . .

Memoirs

We talked earlier on about biographies and memoirs being popular, feeding our insatiable need to read about people. We enjoy them in so many different ways: to watch how far the great have fallen with a little well-deserved schadenfreude; out of genuine curiosity about other people, their lives, their decisions, their experiences.

But there's another reason to read about other people: for inspiration.

With all of the bad things that happen in the world, despite all the headlines that tell us of the evils of humanity, there are still people who have lived through some terrible event in history (or have not) and have faced adversity with dignity, courage, kindness. If it's not too cliché to mention them, some of the names that come to mind include Bruno Bettelheim, Elie Wiesel, and Victor Frankl. Their words make a time alive that should never be forgotten. Beyond that, though, their *responses* to the events around them make us want to be better, more, than what we are. In the same way, reading the diaries of Anne Frank can provide the same kind of inspiration for young people.

These voices are important, and in many ways more authentic than the history books which purport to teach us about the era. Josephine Tey has pointed out that history lies not in accounts, but in account books: in the lives of those who lived in. And in an age where history books appear more and more to be written by committee, with little voice, the past comes alive when we can see it through others' eyes, hear it through others' words . . . and ask ourselves if we would live as well as they did, under the circumstances.

Or even under our circumstances. The best gift of others' accounts of their lives and activities is inspiration—is, in fact, a way to open our hearts.

When you read about someone's bravery and courage, someone's selfless act, someone's kindness to others, it affects you. You might close the book, but you don't close your mind or your heart to the story it told. You think about how well these people lived, and there's part of you that sits up a little straighter, that resolves to live a little better, because of it.

What you take into your mind, you also take into your heart. And these words make you better for having read them.

Knowledge Is Power

The reality is the American education system is not very good in terms of imparting general culture and knowledge to students.

How do I know this? Because when I tell people that my last name is spelled the same as that of Paul Cézanne, the artist (or the painter, or even the Impressionist), four out of five people give me blank looks or an even blanker "huh?" Anecdotal evidence, but very strong nonetheless.

Of course there are myriad other reasons to be fearful for our collective future in terms of how we're educating our children; let's look at what can be done about it. And I'm not just talking about your children; I'm talking about *you*.

While it can be argued that a great deal of useful discourse goes on inside a classroom, the fundamentals still are this: books are read. Yes, their ideas are discussed, hopefully under the guidance of someone who knows more about the subject than anyone else in the room; at its most fundamental level, a lot of education comes down to reading books.

So . . . why not read them? You, sitting there: why not read them?

The stacks of your local public library and the shelves of your local bookshop are filled with enough information to keep you learning forever. Start by taking a stroll around either one of them. Give yourself enough time, so that you're not thinking ahead to your next appointment or task. Chances are you've never done this, or haven't done it much: people generally either browse in a familiar section amid familiar authors, or they look up precisely the book they want, go to it, and leave. I'm talking about an expedition, here: get to know the library or bookshop.

Start with a map, as good explorers do. The reference or circulation desk of the library will have one; in bookshops they're not generally available on paper, but there's often one visible that you can copy (you did bring a notebook and pen with you, right?), or ask a bookseller to help you put one together.

Also be prepared. As mentioned above, have a notebook and pen with you. If your mind is at all curious, you're going to have a great many titles and notes to jot down. I've been in the stacks at the library and felt, sometimes, that I was drowning in wonder: so many subjects I wanted to read about, so many authors yet unfamiliar to me, so many titles to go on my "to be read" list! So be prepared.

Start with a quick walk-through to familiarize yourself with the layout of the books. In a library this is a straightforward affair, although quirks of architecture can make it tricky at times. I frequent two public libraries on a regular basis: that of Manchester, New Hampshire, and that of Provincetown, Massachusetts. And while the Manchester library is a grand affair of marble balustrades, a rotunda, and a logical layout, the library in Provincetown moved into a space that was originally a church and subsequently a museum that featured a three-quarters-sized model of an early fishing boat called the *Rose Dorothea*. The model is in the middle of the building and books, bookcases, tables and people have to flow around it. That presents some interesting organizational challenges, to say the least!

Every library is unique. Every library has its own ethos, its own flavor. Get to know yours.

In a bookshop, there may be a less obvious organizational structure, but once you've seen the layout a few times, you should be able to navigate it with ease.

Once you've had your initial tour, I'm going to suggest that you spend this first visit (which one hopes will be the first of several) in the following way:

- go to the "current affairs" section. This can be tricky: it's sometimes located in the sociology section, sometimes not.

- look through the subsections, which will probably include current affairs, women's studies, African American studies, Asian studies, gay studies, Latino studies, etc.

- browse this section. Pick up one or two books out of each of them.

Take a couple of hours and do this once a week at first. Change sections: try history. Try inspiration. Try science. You may be amazed at what you discover.

This section is titled "knowledge is power." And that's really what it's about: not having power over anything, but feeling the power inside yourself that we talked about back at the beginning of this book when we met the Wapiti-Hoo: "every part of him is filled with the joy of knowing everything that he knows." To know things in that joyful way; to feel connections with the people and the world around you, to see all of life as one shining tapestry and knowing and understanding the dazzling threads that bring it to life—this is what reading can bring you.

Yes, I know what you're thinking, and you're absolutely right.

It's all about flying away.

READING EXERCISE

Pick a topic. Any topic.

Geology. Astronomy. The Civil Rights movement. Terraforming. Greenwich Village. Impressionist art. Motorcycles. Information technology. Mythology. Architecture. String Theory. Death.

Or anything else that your heart desires. Try to choose something that you don't know much about. Now choose a book (bibliographies are available online or *chez* your local library).

Don't read it yet!

First you want to center yourself. Take a deep breath in, filling your lungs from the bottom up. Hold it. Release it slowly, again trying to empty out every last bit of air. Hold that again before breathing in.

Think about why you're looking at this topic. Are there ways in which it might enrich your life? Will it help you understand something you've long been wondering about? Or will it, simply, give you joy in knowing about it?

Any answer is the right answer. Your answer is the right answer. Hold that answer in your mind now, and open the book.

Every time you mark your page and put the book down, remind yourself of your thoughts. Have your motivations for reading changed as you've gotten into the book? Or are you finding it frustrating, difficult to access? Sit with those feelings for a while, too.

Keep checking in with yourself as you're reading: try to be aware of yourself reading, of interacting with the subject matter and the way it's being communicated. This is a dialogue: what is your part in it?

How can this book help you fly away?

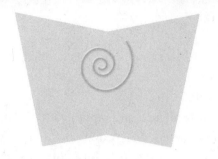

Conclusion

As I conclude this book, I have a confession to make. My introduction to the classics of literature—at least in literature read in English—didn't happen in a library or a schoolroom.

I stole a book.

It was my mother's, and I stole it because she told me I couldn't read it yet. I didn't need much more incentive than that. I was nine years old, and we were living in a fairy-tale house near the Bois de Boulogne in Paris, filled with thin Persian rugs and rich polished antiques and lush greenery—it was a little like living in the middle of an Edwardian novel but without the vapors. My bedroom-cum-study was at the top of several flights of stairs, with windows overlooking the slate rooftops around us, and a secluded "secret" (yeah, right) window seat. And it was there that I curled up with my contraband and a bar of Toblerone chocolate and first read about Melville and Shakespeare and Sir Walter Scott.

The book was *The Classics Reclassified* by the very funny and talented Richard Armour, and it was a sort of tongue-in-cheek cheat sheet for a number of Very Important Books. I remember in particular the beginning of Armour's account of Shakespeare's *Julius Caesar:* "The scene is Rome: A street. A street was, presumably, just north of B Street."

You get my drift.

Armour introduced each author, talked about one book by that author, and even included a "quiz" at the end of each account (which I, of course, dutifully took, not quite getting that the questions were rhetorical and actually very, very funny). It was an amazingly bizarre start to a lifetime of reading and loving those books and others like them, books both within and outside the Western canon of Very Important Books.

But what continues to amaze me, decades later, is this: he didn't do such a bad job. I still haven't read *The Scarlet Letter*, and, frankly, don't feel a pressing need to do so. I've read other books written by Nathanial Hawthorne, and I have that wonderful tongue-in-cheek Armour version of Hester Prynne and Roger Chillingworth and the Reverend Dimmesdale and Pearl (and, cross my heart, I promise I didn't just look up those characters' names, I remembered them . . . from Richard Armour!) and their issues and actions to go by.

I know in a sense that's like admitting that I read the abbreviated, abridged versions available to students desperate to not actually read their assigned texts; the truth is, though, that *The Classics Reclassified* was a lot of fun. And when I did actually read the other books, I met them as old friends. I struggled through reading the "real" Moby-Dick with Richard Armour twinkling at my side ("Call me Ishmael—he'd never liked the name Herman"), and his presence enriched my reading.

I'm telling you this not because I feel a need for soul-cleansing, but rather as a bit of a cautionary tale. I read this utterly foolish, utterly wonderful book at a very formative time in my life, and grew into a person who loves books, loves stories, loves to read, a person, in fact, who makes her living with words. Inspiration is found in odd and unexpected places, and we shouldn't be too quick to judge the circuitous routes that some may take to reach the same destination.

For example, we have the plethora of movies that have been adapted from novels. How many times have you read a book, then watched the movie, then subsequently said (with your face screwed up as though you'd just smelled something awful), "Oh, the book was so much better!"? Come on: tell the truth. Raise your hand. Don't be afraid.

The truth is, we all have. I have. You have. And usually it's true, even though our motives for pointing it out may not be completely pure (I'm a literary snob who only consented to go to this movie because my boyfriend insisted and it turned out exactly as I said it would and people who watch movies instead of reading the book are morally inferior to those of us who read).

But here's the thing. Not everybody grew up snuggling with Richard Armour on a window seat. Not everybody came from a family that treasured books and encouraged reading. Hell, a whole lot of people out there were born into families that either did not or *could* not read.

So the next time you make that face after voicing your oh-so-serious pronouncement as to the relative merits of a film adaptation versus its literary predecessor, stop and think for a moment that it's just possible that some people are doing it the other way around. Inspired by a movie he liked, that person may go find the book . . . and read it. And then maybe read another. Stranger things have happened.

It's not just the movies, either. We're surrounded by alternate paths to enlightenment. There's never *ever* just one way (much less one "right" way) to do things. Here's one: for those of you who don't like it, think before you complain too much about rap music of the people whose hearts may have been opened to poetry through it. It may not be your idea of poetry, but if it's doing what poetry does at its best, lift the individual out of the mundane, even for a brief shining moment . . . then a heart has been opened. And that's all good, as my stepdaughter Anastasia would say.

As I'm finishing up this book, I happen to be in Bucharest, and I'm astonished at how well the publishing industry is doing here; far better than it is doing at home. Romanians read. They don't watch as much television as USians do, and they *read*. They lived through a totalitarian regime until seventeen years ago: they're still enthralled with the fact that they *can*. Read, that is. Whatever they want. Whenever they want. It's amazing to see people still that are amazed by books.

If you didn't read it before—or even if you did—take a moment and go back and read the interviews with Sharon Darling and Lady Di. Take a moment to think about how many people cannot read. Yeah, yeah, you're thinking. Okay, so a lot of people can't read. Let's move on.

Not so fast. Most of the daily activities of Western society are predicated upon reading. Certainly computer literacy is predicated on being able to read, and if you don't like what the digital divide is doing to society, think for a minute about what the literacy divide is doing. It creates a subclass of people, people who cannot access decent jobs, decent living arrangements—not to mention the wonders that *you* know are locked inside of the books you don't give a second thought to.

I met Anastasia before she learned to read. From her I got a glimpse of and began to understand the wonder of the written word, the treasures that it unlocks. I'll never forget the longing in her voice when she said that she wished she could read, and the despair she felt—and voiced, eloquently!—when she believed that she never would be able to. That brought me back in touch with the essentials, with the whole world one can suddenly access if one can read . . . and with how that world is nothing but a closed door if one cannot.

If reading does open your heart, if anything you've read in this book has resonated with you in any way, then I urge you to take it one step further and think seriously about promoting literacy. It can be as simple as going to the online literacy site (at theliteracy site.com) and clicking to help fund books for children, or as involved as volunteering at your local library or literacy center to help teach an adult to read.

If you're reading this now, it probably means that you take reading for granted. There are millions of people worldwide who do not, and hundreds of them live in your community. Wouldn't it be a magical thing to be able to open someone else's heart with reading?

Go to your Internet browser and enter "literacy" into the search field and watch the number of programs that come up. You can also find some of them in the resources section at the end of this book. Consider donating to one of them. Find out what your local literacy programs are doing (a call to your library or city hall can probably help you identify them) and consider volunteering.

Share the magic. Help someone else . . . *fly away.*

I care not how humble your bookshelf may be,
nor how lonely the room which it adorns.
Close the door of that room behind you,
shut off with it all the cares of the outer world,
plunge back into the soothing company of the great dead,
and then you are through the magic portal . . .

—Arthur Conan Doyle

More Numbers

Some lists are just meant to go in appendices. The chapter on plots —*The Butler Did It*—takes on many of the differing thoughts regarding types and numbers of plots available to writers and readers.

But, wait, there's more!

20 Plots

Ronald B. Tobias, in his book *20 Master Plots,* proposes (as you've probably ascertained from the title) twenty basic plots:

1. Quest

2. Adventure

3. Pursuit

4. Rescue

5. Escape

6. Revenge

7. The Riddle

8. Rivalry

9. Underdog

10 Temptation

11. Metamorphosis

12. Transformation

13. Maturation

14. Love

15. Forbidden Love

16. Sacrifice

17. Discovery

18. Wretched Excess

19. Ascension

20. Descension.

36 Plots

What's sixteen better than twenty? That would be Georges Polti's *The Thirty-Six Dramatic Situations.*

Polti doesn't claim his list to be original; he maintains that it's none other than Goethe who came up with thirty-six plots that he feels are the central plots of all literature:

1. Supplication (in which the supplicant must beg something from power in authority)

2. Deliverance

3. Crime pursued by vengeance

4. Vengeance taken for kindred upon kindred

5. Pursuit

6. Disaster

7. Falling prey to cruelty of misfortune

8. Revolt

9. Daring enterprise

10. Abduction

11. Enigma (temptation or a riddle)

12. Obtaining

13. Enmity of family

14. Rivalry of family

15. Murderous adultery

16. Madness

17. Fatal imprudence

18. Involuntary crimes of love (example: discovery that one has married one's mother, sister, etc.)

19. Slaying of a family member

20. Self-sacrifice for an ideal

21. Self-sacrifice for family

22. All sacrificed for passion

23. Necessity of sacrificing loved ones

24. Rivalry of superior and inferior

25. Adultery

26. Crimes of love

27. Discovery of the dishonor of a loved one

28. Obstacles to love

29. An enemy loved

30 Ambition

31. Conflict with God

32. Mistaken jealousy

33. Erroneous judgment

34. Remorse

35. Recovery of a lost one

36. Loss of loved ones.

APPENDIX B

Plot Twists and Turns

A conversation with Odile Sullivan-Tarazi was too good to not include here. "In *Poetic Closure: A Study of How Poems End*," she writes, "Barbara Herrnstein Smith discusses the technique of the surprise ending—what works, what doesn't, and why—at great length. She says that the surprise ending that works provides a perspective from which we can appreciate 'a significant pattern, principle, or motive' that we had not seen before. A disappointing ending, by contrast, reveals nothing of significance, nothing of the structure. In terms of technique, the disappointing ending (she says) may too readily or in too lockstep a fashion complete the causal sequence, or it may not sufficiently have been prepared for. It fails because as an ending it remains unjustified: narrative expectations are neither successfully met nor overturned.

"Frank Kermode's *The Sense of an Ending* offers another classic discussion. He explores the twist that sets the story going, as well as the twist that often closes it. Of the action that sets the story going, he says, for instance: 'The more daring the peripeteia, the more we may feel that the work respects our sense of reality; and the more certainly we shall feel that the fiction under consideration is one of those which, by upsetting the ordinary balance of our naïve expectations, is finding something out for us, something *real*.'

"In *The Rhetoric of Fiction,* speaking in a similar vein, Wayne Booth notes that '[a]ll good works surprise us, and they surprise us largely by bringing to our attention convincing cause-and-effect patterns which were earlier played down.' He too discusses the way in which the endpoint—the point from which we review events and finally understand the entire story—works in concert with surprise."

Resources

(Annotated as appropriate)

This is an extremely limited list. How can anyone do justice to all the resources that could enhance one's experience of reading? I've chosen instead to point you toward a very few resources that I've found useful, liked, use, etc., and hope that you'll continue to build your own set of resources as you explore the world of literature.

Books

About Books

Every Book Its Reader: The Power of the Printed Word to Stir the World (Nicholas Basbanes): A wonderful volume that looks at writings that fire imaginations and make things happen in the world. Basbanes believes that literature can train physicians, nurture children, and rehabilitate criminal offenders. Whether you agree with him or not, his arguments are guaranteed to make you think.

On Reading (Marcel Proust): Written in 1906 and still filled with marvelous truths and truisms for today.

Fairy Tales

Fairy Tale in the Ancient World (Graham Anderson): The author associates fairy tales that the modern world thinks of as belonging to it, but which in fact come from much earlier oral (and sometimes written) traditions. Interestingly, he looks at the level of violence and cruelty in the stories to claim that they were originally intended for adults, something that has long been a contention of *this* author!

Fairy Tales from Before Fairy Tales: The Medieval Latin Past of Wonderful Lies (Jan M. Ziolkowski): It's a wonderful book. Don't be put off by the "medieval Latin past" bit—you'll be surprised by a lot of what is here.

Plots, Stories, and Other Devices

The Seven Basic Plots (Christopher Booker): Booker makes a good argument that is well illustrated for his contention that there are seven. See what you think.

How-To Books

How To Read and Why (Harold Bloom): Whether or not one accepts Bloom as an arbiter of literature, this book is well worth reading. He goes through material by genres (short stories, poetry, novels, etc.) but also has a wonderful introduction titled, "Why Read?" Why, indeed? Read this and find out.

How to Read Literature Like a Professor (Thomas C. Foster)

How to Read a Novel (John Sutherland)

Teaching the World to Read (Frank C. Laubach)

Plots

"Forms of the Plot" (N. Friedman) and "The Concept of the Plot" (R. S. Crane), in *The Theory of the Novel* (E. Stevick)

Other

Dreamtime: Concerning the Boundary between Wilderness and Civilization, by Hans Peter Duerr: An intelligent discussion of the willingness/ unwillingness of certain authors and scholars to step out of their shoes and try to "walk" in those of others in order to attain a true view of others' lives. Duerr points out that most writing has (due to a lack of respect, serious personal effort and willingness to understand) often little or nothing to do with foreign ways of life. Real contacts with anything "other" are generally avoided out of fear of losing both one's identity and the acceptance of the scientific community.

The Ritual Process, by Victor Turner: Here is the first and most complete writing about liminality. Turner coined the term and his is still, to my mind, the best explanation of it.

Byron and the Shelleys: The story of a friendship, by Jane Blumberg. Excellent survey.

Vampyres: Lord Byron to Count Dracula, by Christopher Frayling. Do yourself a favor. Reserve a Saturday night to be alone, procure either a very excellent wine or an equally excellent tea, and indulge in this book. Don't bother locking the door. It won't help.

Films Derived From Books

Gothic (film directed by Ken Russell, 1986) Did you know this film is one huge quote from various sources, genuine and speculative? There must be five minutes of original dialogue in it. Amazing. And still—something of a classic.

Haunted Summer (film directed by Ivan Passer, 1988). Another version of the events of 1816 described earlier in this book.

Websites

"Flood Stories from Around the World," by Mark Isaak (talkorigins. org/faqs/flood-myths.html): This is the study referenced in chapter two, amazing in scope and fascinating in detail. I have lost several hours on this site; you may, too!

The world and languages of J. R. R. Tolkien come to life at uib.no/ people/hnohf, a site designed and maintained by a Norwegian who learned Hebrew for the fun of it, which should tell you everything.

When I was researching spirituality and books, I came across this website that addresses the often-misguided attempts by nonnative people to try and adopt native spirituality at native-languages.org/religion.htm. His experience:

> Since I have put this page up, I have received many anguished emails saying "But my grandmother was part Cherokee . . . are you telling me to just forget that part of myself? How can I honor my Native ancestors if you won't share your religion with me?" The answer is simple: honor them the way they would want to be honored. Don't pay some new-age guru $250 to perform fake "Native American" rituals that would have offended your ancestors, go physically to their tribe and re-connect with their other descendants. It will be hard work convincing the people there that you are genuine but if you go with humility and patience you will eventually be accepted, and that is the ONLY way you will ever become part of the spiritual tradition you desire. There is no shortcut to that. Native spirituality belongs only to the cultural group, and anyone who tells you otherwise is trying to make some money off of you and/or to take a power trip at your expense.

"Library Thing" (at librarything.com) is an online cataloging utility for the books you read. It's also a networking tool where you can connect to others who have read the same books. This is for those among you who like to keep an ongoing catalog of the books you've read; it's a way to keep that catalog online, searchable, and as public as you'd like it to be. It's free for up to 200 books, or $10/year for more. There's also a $25/life option.

The "Online Books" page (onlinebooks.library.upenn.edu) lists over 25,000 free books on the Web and includes not only an index of thousands of books that are available online, but also pointers to significant directories and archives, and special features such as the Celebration of Women Writers and a list of banned books online.

If you read the conclusion and want to become involved in literacy work, a good place for you to start is at the "Literacy Directory" (literacydirectory.org), a database created and maintained by the National Institute for Literacy and Partners. You may also wish to visit the National Institute for Literacy's own site at nifl.gov.

Download a report on literacy in America at nces.ed.gov/pubs93/93275.pdf.

"Reading is Fundamental" is at rif.org/about/programs/default.mspx and "offer(s) enriching activities that spark children's interest in reading. And every child involved with RIF gets to choose and keep new books, at no cost to the children or their families."

The National Center for Family Literacy (the program referred to in one of the interviews) is at famlit.org. "Literacy is the change agent that inspires families and communities to raise the achievement bar. Family is the conduit for long-lasting, meaningful change. Working together with families, communities and dedicated partners, NCFL's services bring about change to ensure that parents and children achieve their goals for success."

The "Internet Public Library" can be found at ipl.org and is very much a **library**. It includes a number of annotated collections, ready reference information (almanacs, dictionaries, encyclopedia), a reading room, a kids' area and a teens' area, special collections, search tools, and the ever-popular Ask A Question feature.

Also check out the "Digital Librarian," where you'll find "a librarian's choice of the best of the Web." Read more at digital-librarian.com.

The "voice of America's libraries" is the "American Library Association" (ala.org), the oldest and largest library association in the world, with more than 64,000 members.

While I'm always anxious for people to give business to their local independent **booksellers**, sometimes when money is tight everyone has to comparison shop. You can do it at "Best Book Buys" (bestweb-buys.com/books) where you can search by author, title, keyword, subject, or even ISBN. Another similar service is "Book Finder" at bookfinder.com.

"BookCrossing" (bookcrossing.com): Books just want to be free! Find out how to catch and release them at BookCrossing, a site that tracks books as they pass from reader to reader.

"Booksense" is a national marketing campaign on behalf of the independent bookstores of America; it's at booksense.com. The Booksense Bestseller List is based on sales from over 350 independent bookstores across America. Booksense 76 Picks is a bimonthly selection of eclectic new books chosen by independent booksellers.

Bowker brings us "BookWire," at bookwire.com, "the Internet resource dedicated to new titles, new authors, and the general scoop on the book industry! Use this site to search book reviews, read about the latest releases, watch author video clips, and learn about upcoming book events."

Tired of playing Charades or Trivial Pursuit(tm)? If you're getting together with other readers, you might enjoy playing Name That First Line: all the opening lines you'll need are available at "First Lines: A Sort of Literacy Test" (people.cornell.edu/pages/jad22).

Style

A checklist for the "Elements of Literary Style" is at this unfortunately long URL: lakesideschool.org/upperschool/departments/english/ErikChristensen/WRITING%20STRATEGIES/LiteraryStyles.htm. (It's probably better to just put the title preceded by "checklist" in the search field of your search engine of choice.)

"Bartleby" is an old friend you can find online at bartleby.com/usage.

The "Apostrophe Protection Society" is one of my favorite sites (probably because it echoes my thoughts and concerns so well!); read all about it at apostrophe.fsnet.co.uk.

Want to learn about world language systems? Then the site you want is "Omniglot" (omniglot.com/writing/index.htm). Warning: go to this site at your own peril: it's a black hole of time you'll never get back.

For discussions of style and anything else that crosses his mind, visit my friend Dick Margulis's blog at ampersandvirgule.blogspot.com

And now for something completely different . . .

I can't leave a list of resources without citing one of my favorite shopping places, Levenger. The company notes that it provides "tools for the serious reader," and indeed it does. Go to levenger.com and request a paper catalog—their merchandise is best viewed like a book, at one's ease rather than hunched over a desk in front of a computer.

. . . and something more different still . . .

Here are some books, ideas, websites that you might want to keep for a rainy day, a day when your horizon feels flat and your usual activities less interesting to you than usual. One of the best ways to wake up your senses, I have found, is by challenging yourself to step away from everything you know and try something different. This can often be accomplished by travel, but as this is a book about reading, let's look at some of the ways you can become a more energetic traveler of the interior:

1. Read some Calvino. In particular, try *If On a Winter's Night a Traveler.* (I've had to try that particular volume, I must admit, more than once.) Calvino led one of the more interesting lives one can imagine, going from fascist to communist and partway back again, rubbing elbows with Che Guevara and Gore Vidal, Roland Barthes and Claude Levi-Strauss in the process, and

being part of several of the twentieth century's major intellectual movements.

2. Read an encyclopedia. Any year will do; any letter of the alphabet will do. If you're doing it online, follow the links. I'll guarantee that you'll find something fascinating to think about.

3. Be inspired by images. There are some wonderful "coffee table" books out there that do show that sometimes pictures can express what words cannot. Or help you to make connection where there weren't any before. Look through the big sale books toward the front of any Barnes & Noble, as an example: lots of different subject areas, lots of images to explore. Books aren't always just about words.

4. Become inspired by words. Go to TheHungerSite.com and click to help feed the hungry, then click through and spend a little time on the literacy site there. Don't just click; think about how these words impact you, how meaningful they can be for your life.

5. Explore a place. Take a map and put a pin in it. Now read everything that you can about that place. What authors lived there? Read their works. Is there a travel guide—either on or offline—about the place? Read it, too. Do a Web search and discover everything that you can about the place. Travel takes place often most profoundly in the mind.

6. Shake things up a little. Read John Barth (*The Floating Opera* is a good place to start). Read Kurt Vonnegut (if you haven't read *Cat's Cradle*, do so now: it was one of his own favorite works). Read Carl Hiaasen. And please, please, please read some Oscar Wilde. Or a lot of Oscar Wilde. If that doesn't make you start looking at things a little differently, nothing will.

7. Read some George Lakoff. The subject of language and linguistics is obviously one very close to my heart. Lakoff, though, expands the discussion into talk about how subject matters are "framed" by the use of semantics, and that should get you thinking. No matter where you live on the political spectrum, you'll find his discussion of how the Republican Party successfully framed issues in the years of the second Bush administration—it's a cautionary tale.

Index

Adventure, 101–103
Aesop's Fables, 96
Aird, Catherine, 88
All Creatures Great and Small, 106
Allende, Isabel, 51
Allingham, Margery, 34
Andrews, Roy Chapman, 64
Angers, France, 75–76
Antiheroes, 58–59
Archetypes, 22, 87
Aristotle, 83
Armour, Richard, 157–158
Ash Wednesday (poem), 125
Asturias, Miguel Ángel, 50–51
At the Back of the North Wind, 89

Bailey, Joseph, 150
Barth, John, 176
Base, Graeme, 10
Beah, Ishmael, 149
Bettelheim, Bruno, 23, 152
Between Silk and Cyanide, 72
Bible, 67

Black Stallion, The, 80
Blake, William, 42, 123
Blatty, William, 35
Bloom, Harold, 103, 136
Blyton, Enid, 32–33
Book genres
    adventure, 43–44
    children, 7–16, 24–25
    coffee table, 176
    exile, 46–48
    fantasy, 50
    gothic, 116–119
    historical, 71–72
    historical fiction, 69–71, 72
    humor, 44–45
    literary fiction, 139–140
    magical realism, 50–51
    memoirs, 55, 151–153
    mystery and crime, 35, 61, 66, 87–92
    nonfiction, 149–155
    popular fiction, 138, 139–140
    scholarly, 149–150
    science fiction, 49–51, 64

self-help, 150–152
short stories, 115
speculative fiction, 76
travel, 44–46, 108, 176
Book groups, 141
Book lists, 109
Book of One Thousand and One Nights, 27–30
Book Thief, The, 104
Bookstores, 153–155
Booth, Wayne, 168
Boundaries, 8–9
Bowles, Paul, 46
Boy and His Dog, A, 94
Bray, Libba, 53
Breakheart Hill, 93
Bryson, Bill, 45
Buchwald, Art, 101
Buckeridge, Anthony, 33
Buddhism, 126, 128–129
Buechner, Frederick, 125–126
Burgess, Anthony,58
Burke, James Lee, 35
Byron, George Gordon, Lord Byron, 119, 122–123

Call the Darkness Light, 72
Calvino, Italo, 175–176
Campbell, Joseph, 23
Campbell, Joseph, 87
Candlelight, 40
Canon, Western, 103, 157–158
Carlson, Richard, 150
Carroll, John, 86
Castle of Otranto, The, 116
Cat's Cradle, 176
Catch-22, 58

Catholicism, 126
Chadwick, Elizabeth, 95–98
Champion Dog: Prince Tom, 64
Chandler, Raymond, 90
Characters, 58–61, 91–92, 141–143
Charlie Parker Played Be Bop, 14
Chatham School Affair, The, 93
Chesnutt, Charles W., 62
Child Called "It," A, 149
Childe Harold's Pilgrimage (poem), 122
Childhood, 7–9, 149
Childhood, A, 149
Christy, 108
Cities and towns. *See* Places.
Classics Reclassified, The, 157
Clockwork Orange, A, 58
Coben, Harlan, 91
Collective unconscious, 22, 87
Connecticut Yankee in King Arthur's Court, A, 76
Conroy, Pat, 58
Conscientious Objector (poem), 103
Cook, Thomas H., 93
Creative Thinking, 131
Creativity, 136, 140–144
Crews, Harry, 149
Crombie, Deborah, 89
Crompton, Richmal, 32, 96
Cryptonomicon, 76
Czarnecki, Anastasia, 53–54

Dance Night, 44
Dark Star Safari: Overland from Cairo to Cape Town, 44

Darling, Sharon, 146–148
Daughter of Time, The, 132
David and the Phoenix, 64
Death, 19, 103–105, 150
Death of the Ball Turret Gunner (poem), 104
December, 40
Detectives, 88–91
Dexter, Colin, 25, 89
Disney, Walt, 135
Doctorow, E. L., 51
Doors of Perception, The, 108
Dostoevsky, Fyodor, 23, 58
Dreaming Darkly Dexter, 58
Dubus, Andre, 59
Dunnett, Dorothy, 96–97

Eagle and the Raven, The, 69–70
Eliade, Mircea, 23
Eliot, T. S., 125
Ellison, Harlan, 94
Ellison, Ralph, 106
Emotions, 81, 89, 111–130
Empathy, 60–62
Encyclopedia Britannica, 64
Endings, surprise, 93–94, 167–168
Epic of Gilgamesh, 19
Escapism, 2–4
Evil, 59
Exorcist, The, 35

Fairy tales, 24–25, 30–31, 169–170
Families, 57–58, 70
Fear, 114–121
Feynman, Richard, 14

Fisher, Walter, 26
Fleming, Ian, 34
Floating Opera, The, 176
Follow My Leader, 64
Formulas, 118
Foster, Thomas, 1
Foster-Harris, William, 84–85
Fowles, John, 35
Francis, Dick, 62, 80
Frank, Anne, 152
Frankenstein, 120–121
Frankl, Victor, 152
Frayn, Michael, 36
Friedman, Norman, 84

Garcia Márquez, Gabriel, 51
Gardner, John, 66
Gedge, Pauline, 69, 70
Gellis, Roberta, 97
George, Elizabeth, 89
Ghost stories, 119–121
Glenn, Louise, 139
Golden Egg Book, 64
Grahame, Kenneth, 105
Green Smoke, 96

Haley, Carolyn, 79–81
Hanshan, 129
Hanta Yo, 98
Harpies, 20
Hart, Alison, 54
Heidi, 96
Heinlein, Robert A., 76, 99
Heller, Joseph, 58
Henry, O., 94
Herbert, Frank, 50
Hiaasen, Carl, 176

Hill, Ruth Beebe, 98
Hillerman, Tony, 61
Histories, personal, 25–27
Holland, Cecilia, 97
Household, Geoffrey, 62
How to Read Literature Like a Professor, 1
How to Survive the Loss of a Love, 150
Hubbard, P. M., 35
Hughes, Langston, 61–62
Hugo, Victor, 113, 123
Huxley, Aldous, 108

I Made a Line, 108
If On a Winter's Night a Traveler, 175
Imagination, 131–144
Immortals Quartet, 54
Injustice, 62, 70
Invisible Man, 106
Ivy Tree, The, 41, 93

Jabberwocky, 10–11
Jackson, Colin, 85
James, P. D., 89
Jarrell, Randall, 103–104
Johnston, Denis, 85–86
Journeys, 19, 28
Julian of Norwich, 125
Jung, Carl, 22–23, 87

Kabbalah, 126
Kabul Beauty School, 102
Kermode, Frank, 167
Khayyam, Omar, 129–130
Kipling, Rudyard, 64, 85, 94

Knowledge, 13–14,151, 153–155
Kotlowitz, Alex, 148
Kundera, Milan, 51

Lady Di, 17–18
Lakoff, George, 177
Landscapes, 36–37
Le Carré, John, 62
LeBoeuf, Michael, 131
Lehane, Dennis, 91, 93
Levenger (store), 175
Lewis, C. S., 7, 64
Leys, 37
Libraries, 153–155, 173
Life, 60–63, 92, 100–103, 106–107, 136–137
Liminality, 8–9
Lindsay, Jeff, 58
Lion, the Witch, and the Wardrobe, The, 7
Literacy, 146–148, 160–161, 173
Long Good-bye, The, 90
Long Way Gone, A, 149
Love, 122–124
Lovecraft, Howard Phillips, 115–116
Lowell, Massachusetts, 72–73
Lyall, Gavin, 44, 62

Macaulay, David, 51
MacDonald, Karen, 107–109
Macdonald, Ross, 90
Magazines, 135–136
Magus, The, 35
Man in the Moss, The, 40
Manning, Rosemary, 96

Margulis, Dick, 175
Mark, Leo, 72
Marshall, Catherine, 108
Maupassant, Guy de, 94
Mayes, Francis, 44
Mayle, Peter, 44
McBain, Ed, 90
Meade, Chris, 140
Memorization, 103, 112, 113–114
Men Like Gods, 76
Merton, Thomas, 128
Michaels, Barbara, 80
Michell, John, 36–37
Millay, Edna St. Vincent, 103
Millions of Cats, 108
Milne, A. A., 64
Mitchell, Elyne, 96
Moon Is a Harsh Mistress, 99
More, Thomas, 132, 133
Motel of the Mysteries, 51
Movies, 159, 171
Murders in the Rue Morgue, The, 88
Music, 134–135, 159
My Father's Dragon, 64
Mysteries of Udolpho, The, 117
Mysticism, 125–126
Myths, 20–23, 87

Nafisi, Azar, 48
Narrative paradigm, 26
National Center for Family Literacy (NCFL), 146
Nivens, Larry, 50
Northam, Jeremy, 57
Notes from the Underground, 58
Nouwen, Henri, 106

O'Craven, Jill, 4–6
O'Craven, Mandy, 4–6
O'Hara, Mary, 96
Open Your Heart with Writing, 60
Opening the Book (organization), 140

Pact, The, 104
Page, Kathy, 76–77
Parker, Charlie, 15
Pearl, Nancy, 90, 133
Phil the Shelf (radio show), 32
Picture books, 13, 14
Pierce, Tamara, 53, 54
Places, 36–37, 39–51, 72–76
Plays, 66
Pleasure of Finding Out, The, 14
Plots, 83–88, 92, 163–166, 170
Poe, Edgar Allan, 88, 104, 114–115
Poetic Closure: A Study of How Poems End, 167
Poetry, 103–105, 114, 122–123, 125, 126–130, 159–160
Polidoro, John, 120
Polti, Georges, 85, 164–166
Powell, Dawn, 44
Pratchett, Terry, 25–26, 93
Prince of Tides, The, 58
Princes in the Tower, The, 132
Professions, 62, 91
Provincetown, Massachusetts, 73–75
Psychology, 115, 120–121

Quests, 19, 20
Quindlen, Anna, 133

Radcliffe, Anne, 117–118
Ramakrishna, 128
Rankin, Ian, 89
Raschka, Chris, 14
Raven, The (poem), 104, 114
Readers' Digest, 135
Reading Lolita in Tehran, 48
Reading, 1–2, 14, 33–34, 99–106,
    111–112, 131–144, 157–161,
    170
    aloud, 11, 14, 16
    books about, 169, 170
    exercises, 16, 30–31, 52, 63,
        78–79, 95, 107, 130,
        144–145, 155–156
    interviews about, 4–6, 17–18,
        31–37, 53–54, 63–67, 79–81,
        95–98, 107–109, 146–148
    resources, 169–177
Relationships, 55–58
Rhetoric of Fiction, The, 168
Rhythm, 15
Rickman, Phil, 31–37, 40, 62
Rodriguez, Deborah, 102
Romeo and Juliet, 104
Rosen, Neil M., 60
Rosenbaum, Daniel, 57
Rubaiyat (poem), 129
Rumi, Jalalud'din, 127
Rushdie, Salman, 51

Sartre, Jean-Paul, 136
Sayers, Dorothy L., 91
Scheherazade (character),
    29–30
Self-discovery, 136–137, 143,
    151

Sense of an Ending, The, 167
Shadow Horse, 54
Shakespeare, William, 104, 123,
    132, 133
Shelley, Mary Wollstonecraft,
    119, 120
Shelley, Percy Bysshe, 119, 123
Sheltering Sky, The, 46
Shetterly, Will, 94
Shreve, Anita, 56–57
Shutter Island, 93
*Shy Stegosaurus of Cricket Creek,
    The*, 64
Simenon, Georges, 90
*Slowing Down to the Speed of
    Life*, 150–151
Smith, Barbara Herrnstein, 167
Smith, John F., 13, 132
Snow Crash, 138
Spirituality, 124–130
Spyri, Johanna, 96
St. John of the Cross, 125
St. Teresa of Ávila, 127
Stephenson, Neal, 76, 87, 138
Stewart, Mary, 41, 80, 93
Stories and storytelling, 10,
    15–16, 19–30, 65–66, 71, 80,
    83–87, 92, 93–94, 96, 138,
    140–143, 147
Strange Fits of Passion, 56
Sufism, 126, 127
Suicide, 104
Sullivan-Tarazi, Odile, 94, 167
Surprises, 93–94

Tall Book of Make-Believe, 10
Tangled Lands, The, 94

Tey, Josephine, 132, 152
Themes, 19–23, 25, 28–29, 87, 149
There Are No Children Here, 148
Theroux, Paul, 44
Thirty-Six Dramatic Situations, The, 164–166
Thoreau, Henry David, 106
Tiger in the Smoke, The, 34
Tobias, Ronald B., 163–164
Todd, Barbara Euphan, 96
Tolkien, J. R. R., 24, 25, 50, 87
Toward the End of the Morning, 36
Travel, armchair, 40–41, 44–46
Triangle, 71
Turner, Victor, 8
TV Humphrey, 64
Twain, Mark, 76, 104, 108
20 Master Plots, 163–164

Under the Tuscan Sun, 44
Until the Sun Falls, 97
Updike, John, 64
Use of Enchantment, The, 23

Van Gogh, Vincent, 124
Van Riel, Rachel, 140
Vendler, Helen, 103
Verne, Jules, 49
View over Atlantis, The, 36–37

Von Drehle, David, 71
Vonnegut, Kurt, 86, 176

Walden, 106
Walpole, Horace, 116
Wapiti-Hoo, The, 11–13, 54
Watkins, Alfred, 37
Weir, Alison, 132
Wells, H. G., 49, 76
Wetmore, Andrew, 63–67
Whitney, Phyllis A., 39
Wiesel, Elie, 152
Wilde, Oscar, 176
Wind in the Willows, The, 96, 105–106
Winnie the Pooh, 96
Wise, Mark, 94
Women, portrayal of, 20, 29–30
Worzel Gummidge, 96
Wrede, Patricia C., 50
Writing, 81
    styles of, 137–139, 174–175

Year in Provence, A, 44
Yeats, William Butler, 42
Young Warriors: Stories of Strength, 54

Zaroulis, Nancy, 72
Zusak, Markus, 104

About the Author

Jeannette Cézanne is a writer and editor who divides her time between Manchester, New Hampshire, and Provincetown, Massachusetts. She has published fiction under a number of different pen names and is president of Customline Wordware, Inc., a company providing business, marketing, and literary writing and editing services to corporate and individual clients.

Contests, new titles, events, news, discussion and feedback. Sign up for your latest chance to win and find out about upcoming books at **www.dreamtimepublishing.com**

OUR COMMUNITY

DreamTime Publishing supports the community by participating regularly in worthwhile fundraising and charitable efforts. Let us know what's important to you, and sign up at **www.dreamtimepublishing.com** to find out what's happening near you.

ONLINE BOOK CLUB AND MORE!

Come by and share in a discussion of the latest books from top authors and leave your feedback on DreamTime Publishing's titles and for our authors. Sign up at **www.dreamtimepublishing.com** to get the latest information.

WHAT'S GOING ON?

Check out our online calendar for events and appearances by DreamTime authors. Sign up at **www.dreamtimepublishing.com** to make sure you don't miss anything!